GRAND SLAMS

of TENNIS

Legends, feuds, tennis dads & one-slam wonders

EAMON EVANS

hardie grant books

MELBOURNE · LONDON

Published in 2014 by Hardie Grant Books

Hardie Grant Books (Australia)
Ground Floor, Building 1
658 Church Street
Richmond, Victoria 3121
www.hardiegrant.com.au

Hardie Grant Books (UK)
5th & 6th Floors
52–54 Southwark Street
London SE1 1UN
www.hardiegrant.co.uk

Cataloguing-in-publication data available from the catalogue
of the National Library of Australia at www.nla.gov.au

Grand Slams of Tennis: Legends, feuds, tennis dads and one-slam wonders
ISBN 9781742708980

Cover design by Josh Durham/Design by Committee
Text design and typesetting by Pauline Haas
Typeset in Bauer Bodoni
Printed and bound in Italy by Elcograf

Acknowledgements

Many thanks to Pam Brewster at Hardie Grant for commissioning this sucker, and to Rihana Ries and Penelope Goodes for editing it.

Love and kisses to Jenny, Henry and Eliza (and pats to Bertie the dog).

Contents

INTRODUCTION

> ❝I have always considered tennis as a combat in an arena between two gladiators who have their racquets and their courage as their weapons.❞ — *Yannick Noah*

Thanks for that, Yannick. I myself believe it's more like a game.

A *good* game, though, I hasten to add—and for a while there, I wasn't half bad. Like most child prodigies, I discovered tennis at the age of six or seven, after coming across an old wooden racquet in the back of a cupboard. After a year or so of hitting a ball against a wall, I enrolled in lessons at my local tennis club, and at ten I started entering tournaments. Passers-by used to marvel at my unconventional service action, while my backhand was hailed by experts as being both 'memorable' and 'unique'.

When I hit sixteen, it was time to turn pro. Or, rather, it would have been but for one slight problem. Unlike most child prodigies, it had slowly emerged, I was in fact deeply crap. The thrill of a well-placed forehand, the rush of a crisp half-volley: both these sensations remain foreign to me, though I can tell you all about double faults. Walt Disney once said, 'All our dreams can come true if we have the courage to pursue them', but believe me, folks, he's wrong.

Fortunately, tennis superstardom wasn't my only childhood dream: I also wanted my very own television. And now that I have one (sorry to boast), I can watch superstars play whenever I want. Which, of course, means that I watch them four times a year. During the Australian Open and the French Open, then during Wimbledon and the US Open.

Most tennis tournaments, let's be honest here, are about as important as pumpkin soup. If your favourite player happens to lose the Paine Webber Classic one week, he's got the Birmingham Open the next. If she happens to miss out on the BNP Paribas Masters, then there's always the Ameritech Cup. Not too many children would dream about winning the Western & Southern Financial Group Women's Open. Or indeed be able to spell the Aegon Classic.

But the Grand Slams, they are different. They are, well, grand. The big four tournaments on the tennis calendar are big in every sense of the word: they feature the most players and they fork out the most prize money; they have the shiniest trophies and the noisiest crowds. To win one is to win a ridiculous number of rankings points—and a ridiculous number of headlines all over the globe. It's at the Grand Slams that reputations are won and lost, and it's at the Grand Slams that legends are made.

So why are they such a big deal? Well, that, my friends, is a complicated question, and for an answer, you'll need to read the whole book. But let's just say that that these four tournaments involve a whole lot of history: a whole lot of great players playing great matches, or having great rivalries or great dummy spits. They involve a whole lot of fans going coo coo bananas, and a whole lot of sex, drugs and fun.

In this book, I give you the best bits of Grand Slam history (along with all the basic whens, wheres and whos). If you want to know how some obscure Bulgarian fared in the 1973 French Open, then Google might just be your go. But if you want to know which world number one 'has always been unfaithful to her boyfriends', then grab a drink, take a seat and read on. In *Grand Slams of Tennis* you'll also discover which player has been in and out of jail, and which one became a nun. You'll learn who liked to play without underpants, and who never changes her socks. You'll hear who slept with whom, who wore a wig and whose game was once held up by a gun.

From bankruptcy and battery to bitchiness and brandy, a great many threads have gone into the tapestry that is the history of tennis. But where exactly did that first thread come from? Who actually invented the thing? It's time to travel back in time to eleventh-century Europe, and find out how the grandest of all games began ...

– 1 –
THE GRAND OLD GAME

The divine birth

In the beginning, God created the heavens and the earth—but who the hell created the tennis? The Bible isn't much help in answering that question and nor, it has to be said, are historians. Some of them would have you believe that the game started with cavemen, who used to hit rocks back and forth with their clubs, while others say that racquet-and-ball games were played in Turkey two or three thousand years ago, before spreading to Europe and beyond.

What none of them say, unfortunately, is 'And what's more, I have proof.' Most likely, this is because none exists. While the word 'racquet' probably comes from *rahat*, an Arabic word meaning 'palm of the hand', that's about it for evidence of the game's possible origins in the Middle East.

Which brings us to the monasteries of medieval France. Whether or not God did indeed create the heavens and the earth, some of His employees definitely helped invent tennis. With nothing to do but pray all day, and try very hard not to masturbate, it's perhaps not all that surprising that some red-blooded God-botherer eventually invented a sport to help pass the time.

A sort of cross between squash and handball, *jeu de paume* was played indoors and didn't involve any racquets—or, necessarily, a net. We don't know too much about the rules (if, indeed, there were many) but we do know that when a player was getting ready to serve, he would cry out 'Here you are!' to alert his opponent, just as a golfer might yell 'Fore!' today. Only, being French, it would come out as *'Tenez!'*, a much snappier, and more adaptable, phrase.

Yes, that's right: 'tennis' is a French word—and our language lesson doesn't stop there. When both players had won three points each, there were no English-speaking monks to say 'all square'. So someone would instead say that the score was *à deux le jeu* ('two points to the game'), a rather cumbersome phrase from which we later got 'deuce'.

The strange score of 'love' may also come from French. Some scholars tell us that it comes from *l'oeuf* ('egg')—eggs being much the same shape as a zero. This theory isn't as far-fetched as it sounds (a 'duck' in cricket started out as a 'duck's egg') but there's just one problem: today's French tennis umpires actually use the word *zéro*. 'Love' most likely came to England just a few centuries ago, when a wave of Dutch immigrants arrived from the Low Countries. A player stuck on zero points, the theory goes, would joke that they played for *lof*—that being a Dutch word for honour and glory.

There is no glory in tennis's scoring system, however, just strange numbers and needless confusion. For the 15–30–40 system, as with so much else that's wrong in life, we must again blame the French. While the leap from love to 15 and then 30 was most likely inspired by a convenient church clock wound by a monk to keep track of the score, it's never been entirely clear why the winner of the next point should then arrive at 40, rather than the infinitely more logical 45. The most common theory is that logic *did* once prevail, but then people simply started saying '40' for short.

Evolution

They were, after all, busy men. By the fourteenth century, *jeu de paume* wasn't just a monk's game. It was beloved by bishops, abbots and prelates—not to mention nobles and kings. Louis IV and the Church both attempted to ban the game, but clearly didn't have much luck. Some accounts say that France had as many as 1800 courts (but then again, some accounts will say anything).

In the delicate hands of French dukes, however, *jeu de paume* slowly became 'real tennis': a game that was played while wearing thick leather gloves, and with a cork ball that weighed roughly 3 ounces (85 grams). Over time, some bright spark added strings (well, sheep's intestines) to the glove—and then a still-brighter spark turned the glove into a racquet.

By the sixteenth century, real tennis was sort of recognisable as tennis, so long as you looked very closely. Think short, squat racquets in long, narrow rooms, then add jagged walls (which the ball was supposed to bounce off) and roofed galleries and five-foot-high nets. 'Of the tenetz to winne or lese a chase, Mai no lif wite er that the bal be ronne,' wrote the medieval poet John Gower, and whatever he meant, it was probably right.

That poem, in case you were wondering, was written in 1400 and it represents the first mention of tennis in English. But by no means was it the last. With England controlling vast chunks of France, the game quickly spread across the Channel and has stayed there ever since. An early King Arthur play has Sir Gawain serve it up against seventeen giants, while *The Second Shepherd's Play* ('a jewel of medieval theatre') sees the Three Wise Men wisely ditch the frankincense, and give baby Jesus a tennis ball instead.

And in a jewel of Elizabethan theatre, Shakespeare's *Henry V*, the Big H is given some tennis balls by the King of France and reacts by declaring war. Seeing the present as an insult—or at least a suggestion that he stick to childish pursuits—Henry goes to battle in Agincourt, and leaves it drenched in blood. 'Tell the pleasant Prince this mock of his hath turn'd his balls to gun stones,' he cries semicoherently, so I guess not everyone's a fan.

The sport of kings

Whether this part of *Henry V* is historically accurate—and quite a few sources say that it might be—there's no doubt that real tennis (or, as it's often known, *royal* tennis) was very much the sport of kings. Dozens of courts were built in the palaces of Europe during the late Middle Ages, and many monarchs became stars at the game.

France's Charles VIII does not perhaps belong in this category. His reign came to an end when he banged his head on the door of his tennis court, fell into a coma and died.

Louis X may not have been a model of athleticism, either. He's said to have died from pneumonia after rashly deciding to try a game outdoors.

At least one Scottish monarch also had mixed success at the game. On 4 February 1437, James I was staying overnight in a Perth monastery when he was told that thirty assassins had managed to break in. Fortunately, there was a way out, through a disused sewer tunnel—and James scurried there as quickly as he could. Unfortunately, it turned out to have been blocked up—to prevent tennis balls from getting lost. The king was quickly captured and killed.

By and large, England's kings have had better luck when it comes to tennis (though the untimely death of one eighteenth-century heir to the throne may have been due to a 'blow upon the stomach from a tennis-ball'.) Henry VIII—a man whose ample stomach could have withstood any number of blows—was a particular fan of the game, building a court at Hampton Court that still survives to this day. Henry also partnered the Holy Roman Emperor in a famous game of doubles against the Prince of Orange and the Marquis of Brandenburg. It's said that Anne Boleyn was watching a game of real tennis when he sent soldiers to arrest her, and that Henry himself was playing a game while his executioner gave her the chop.

Even as a corpse, however, Anne Boleyn probably would have been a better player than Charles II. The diarist Samuel

Pepys hated 'to see how the King's play was extolled, without any cause at all ... It was a very loathsome sight.'

By the time of the French Revolution, of course, pretty much *every* monarch was considered a very loathsome sight. The political upheaval that destroyed royal power ironically began on a royal tennis court. When, on 20 June 1789, the chosen representatives of France's commonfolk were banned from representing them at the Estates-General, they got together for a quick meeting at Versailles' tennis court, the largest room they could find nearby. There, in that very room, 576 of the 577 representatives swore an oath to pursue liberty.

They later put the 577th guy in prison.

Real tennis goes outdoors

For a while there, real tennis wasn't all that much more popular than the French royal family, and it came just about as close to death. The game waned in England throughout the first half of the nineteenth century, and in France it was barely played at all. The drop in popularity was mostly due to a space issue. In a post-revolutionary world of good old *égalité*, who could afford to build huge palaces with big rooms designed just for a sport?

But in 1850, the game had a good year. And it was all thanks to a man named Goodyear. Best known for the car tyre company that sprang up years later and cannily borrowed his name, Charles Goodyear invented a way to convert natural rubber into the durable, bendy stuff that we all use today. Bouncier balls were one immediate result — a development which hastened the birth of *jeu de paume*'s bastard children, the indoor games racquetball and squash.

But with such bouncy balls, as many soon noted, who needs to stay indoors? For the first time, a form of tennis could be played on good old grass. And with so many flat, clipped croquet courts scattered all over England, a new sport called *lawn* tennis very soon was.

Some say that the first people to play lawn tennis were Major Harry Gem, a Birmingham solicitor, and his friend Augurio Perera, a merchant from Spain. They certainly played something close to it during the 1860s on a croquet lawn somewhere in Edgbaston. And, along with two local doctors, both men can be credited with starting the world's first tennis club, in 1874 at Leamington Spa.

But the *rules* of the game that we call tennis today probably owe a lot more to another army type, the nicely named Walter Wingfield. Only he called the game Sphairistike. Anxious to make a quick buck (and then ideally a few thousand more), Major Wingfield published a rule book in 1873 for a new game which he named after a Greek phrase meaning 'playing at ball'. As far as the good major was concerned, this meant that he owned any type of racquet game that was played outdoors, and that everyone who played it therefore owed him a fee.

As far as everyone else was concerned, he could get stuffed. And for that matter, so could most of his game. But while today's lawn tennis is not played on an hourglass-shaped court, it does owe many of its rules to that eight-page rule book. Wingfield may not have made any money, but he definitely earned our thanks.

Tennis's remaining refinements — second serves, the rectangular court, the three-foot-three-inch net) came about four years after Sphairistike, thanks to a little croquet club that had broken its lawn roller. Anxious to purchase a new one (and God knows, those things don't come cheap), the All England Croquet Club in Worple St, Wimbledon decided to raise some funds by hosting a tennis tournament. A committee was set up to codify the rules, and the rules that they eventually came up with are those of the game we all play today.

Amateur hour

Having said that, things were still a bit different. That first Wimbledon Gentlemen's Singles Championship in 1877 had just twenty-two gentlemen playing, all up. Each one a man wearing slacks and a blazer, a long-sleeved shirt and a tie. Plus a straw hat, of course, and minus the guinea that he had to fork out to play. No matches were scheduled for the third and fourth days, as no-one wanted to miss the Eton and Harrow cricket match, and fewer than 200 spectators attended in total. Sitting in a three-row grandstand, they saw a cricketer named Spencer Gore become the world's first Wimbledon champion—a feat that at least impressed *them*. Gore himself later ditched tennis for squash, declaring that lawn tennis was 'boring and will never catch on'.

But catch on, tennis soon did. The first US National Men's Singles Championships were held in affluent Newport, Rhode Island, in 1881, and France followed suit just ten years later. The sport featured in the first modern Olympic Games in 1896, and what we now call the Australian Open kicked off nine years after that. It arrived hot on the heels of the first International Lawn Tennis Challenge, a tournament now known as the Davis Cup.

The Davis Cup was so-called because of Dwight Davis, a wealthy Ivy League preppy type–turned–Republican politician, who generously paid for the big silver cup. He also provided us with a pretty good example of the original tennis fan. While real tennis had been the sport of kings, lawn tennis was the sport of the rich. It was a pastime for gentlemen in crisp white slacks, and ladies in the latest frocks—a genteel game played by genteel people in private manors and country clubs.

And when you already have plenty of money, there's no need to try and win more. The Anglo-American elite of the late nineteenth century all loved the idea of the 'gentleman amateur'—the red-blooded sportsman who plays for the ruddy-cheeked joy of it, uncorrupted by the pursuit of cash. Tennis tournaments therefore weren't played for prize money. Indeed, you had to stump up to enter them. Anyone who ever sought to profit from the game could pack up their racquet and play something else.

In 1926, however, 'corruption' arrived. It took the form of an American entrepreneur called CC Pyle. By this time, tennis had spread to the middle (and even—gasp!—lower) classes, thanks to the increasing number of public courts. But not all of the new players wanted to be gentlemen; some, after all, were women, while many of the others wanted to eat.

By flashing some cash, Yankee-style, CC Pyle was able to entice many of Europe's best players across the Atlantic to play in a series of exhibition matches. Every player involved immediately ceased to be an amateur, and was thus banned from Wimbledon and the like. But that didn't stop other players turning professional as the decades rolled by.

Thus began the great divide. From 1926 until 1968, when the tour became open to both amateurs and pros, many of the game's big players were banned from playing the game's big tournaments, because they wanted to play for big money instead. That's why any pre-Open Era record always comes with a caveat: would Player X really have won Grand Slam Y if players A and B had been competing as well?

The Open Era

In 1968, I am pleased to report, tennis officials finally realised that it was 1968, and the amateur ideal was given the boot. The Grand Slams were now open to all, and offered prize money—which all were happy to take. Other amateur tournaments started offering prize money as well, while some simply couldn't and faded away. In 1972, the Association of Tennis Professionals (ATP) was formed to make sense of the chaos, and the Women's Tennis Association (WTA) followed the next year. Both organisations quickly established professional world 'tours' composed of 800 or so tournaments, giving each tournament a set number of 'ranking points' using an exciting new technology called 'computers'.

And the tennis became pretty exciting as well.

With all the best tournaments now featuring all the best players, all and sundry started coming to watch. Standards rose, attendance figures rose—and prize money, sponsorship and TV ratings all started soaring as well. The 1970s are generally seen as tennis's golden age, with big personalities ushering in ever bigger crowds, and millions of tennis courts built all over the globe.

For some of us, the game's lustre has dimmed a little since then, and an engineer named Howard Head is largely to blame. Known to his critics as Dick, Head was a man who had made millions making aluminium snow skis, and then saw an opportunity to make millions more. That opportunity was *aluminium racquets*. Almost twice as large as traditional wooden racquets, Head's Prince racquets revolutionised tennis by making it twice as easy to produce speed and top spin.

'Larger racquets have taken the subtlety out of the game,' is how tennis historian Robert Holland describes the post-Prince era of whack, bang, smash, boom—and plenty of people agree. 'They have made the game much more one-dimensional,' says former champ Angela Mortimer. 'A different kind of talent is now required.'

A more boring kind of talent? Well, it's true enough that today's champions don't seem to have much use for angles, and rarely bother with slices and lobs. Drop shots are increasingly rare; even volleys may soon belong to the past. Why try to out-think your opponent when you can simply out-hit them instead?

But cheer up, Angela, and come on, Robert, there's really no need to frown. If the history of tennis has taught us anything, it's that these things always evolve.

And that the Grand Slams are always worth watching.

THE GRAND SLAMS

Professional tennis players have well over 800 tournaments to choose from to ply their trade. Professional tennis watchers only have four.

Also known as the Majors, the four Grand Slam tournaments are to tennis what John, Paul, George and Ringo were to the Beatles. Yes, tennis has other tournaments, just as the Beatles had producers and roadies. The point is that they belong in the background. Only the Grand Slams should take centre stage.

In part, this is just a question of numbers. There's a reason why the Australian Open (which starts in Melbourne in January), the French Open (Paris, May), Wimbledon (London, June) and the US Open (New York, August) are the only four tournaments on the calendar that last for a solid fortnight. It's because they're the only ones with 128 players. The four Grand Slams feature the most players, the most prize money and the most rankings points, and they get far and away the most media attention.

But the biggest part of the equation is history: Grand Slams also offer the greatest prestige.

The Grand Slam story began in 1924, almost two decades after the Australian Open—the newest of the four tournaments—first got underway. Faced with a need to update the ranking system (though the word 'system' may be overly generous), the International Lawn Tennis Federation declared that, as Australia, France, Great Britain and the USA were the only four countries to have won the Davis Cup at that point, the biggest tournament held in each would henceforth constitute the biggest four in the world.

The four tournaments became known as the 'Grand Slams' in 1933, when Australia's Jack Crawford took out the first three of them, and was on the verge of winning in New York. Journalist John Kieran wrote a widely quoted article to the effect that, if Crawford was to take out the title, it would be a feat comparable to 'a contract to win all 13 tricks in bridge'. (Apparently, this achievement is known as a grand slam. Though I couldn't tell you what a trick is. Or what a contract is, come to think of it).

Unfortunately, Crawford didn't win the Grand Slam, losing the final final to Britain's Fred Perry. But it didn't take long before somebody did. In 1938, the lanky Don Budge made it his mission to win the Grand Slam: 'I looked at the history books, and saw that nobody had won the four major tournaments in one year. Not Tilden, Borotra, Cochet, Lacoste, or Perry. So I started the year with this in mind.' And he ended it without losing a match.

Since Budge's historic accomplishment, only one man and three women have managed to replicate it: Rod Laver in 1962 and 1969, Maureen Connolly in 1953, Margaret Court in 1970, and Steffi Graf in 1988. That's not many. And we may well never see another one. With the Slams now played on four different surfaces, which require different strengths, winning all four has become harder than ever.

But let's not get preoccupied with *the* Grand Slam, folks. Winning *a* Grand Slam tournament is still pretty damn good. After all, John, Paul and George all had very fine solo careers. And Ringo managed to marry a Bond girl.

Calendar-year Grand Slams

1938   Don Budge (USA)
1953   Maureen Connolly (USA)
1962   Rod Laver (Australia)
1969   Rod Laver (Australia)
1970   Margaret Court (Australia)
1988   Steffi Graf (Germany)

Most Grand Slam titles: men

17   Roger Federer (Switzerland)
14   Pete Sampras (USA)
13   Rafael Nadal (Spain)
12   Roy Emerson (Australia)
11   Björn Borg (Sweden), Rod Laver (Australia)
10   Bill Tilden (USA)
8   Andre Agassi (USA), Jimmy Connors (USA), Ivan Lendl (Czechoslovakia, USA), Fred Perry (UK), Ken Rosewall (Australia)
7   Henri Cochet (France), Novak Djokovic (Serbia), René Lacoste (France), William Larned (USA), John McEnroe (USA), William Renshaw (UK), Richard Sears (USA), Mats Wilander (Sweden)
6   Boris Becker (Germany), Don Budge (USA), Jack Crawford (Australia), Stefan Edberg (Sweden), Tony Wilding (Australia)

Most Grand Slam titles: women

24   Margaret Court (Australia)
22   Steffi Graf (Germany)
19   Helen Wills (USA)
18   Chris Evert (USA), Martina Navratalova (Czechoslovakia, USA), Serena Williams (USA)
12   Billie Jean King (USA)
9   Maureen Connolly (USA), Monica Seles (Yugoslavia)
8   Molla Mallory (Norway)
7   Maria Bueno (Brazil), Dorothea Chambers (UK), Evonne Goolagong (Australia), Justine Henin (Belgium), Venus Williams (USA)

Wimbledon

'For me, and most of the other players too, if you had to pick one of the four Grand Slams, you would pick Wimbledon. It's got tradition, it's got atmosphere and it's got mystique.'

Those words came from the mouth of Stefan Edberg, but I could have attributed them to just about anyone. Wimbledon is easily the grandest of the Grand Slams. It's the one everyone wants to win. 'They act like they've got the biggest tournament in the world,' Pete Sampras once said of the famously snooty All England Lawn Tennis and Croquet Club, 'and they're right, they do.'

But does biggest necessarily mean *best*? Played, as it is, on grass—a fast, skidding surface with minimal bounce—it's not exactly a great tournament if you like long, complex rallies. Points at Wimbledon are generally short and the people who win them tend to be tall. Historically speaking, if you take a big enough serve to this south London stadium, there's a good chance that you'll take home a trophy. But if you've just got a good baseline game, you probably won't. A handful of big-serving superstars (Graf, King, the Williams sisters, King, Sampras, Federer, Borg) have won no less than forty-six trophies between them, while the likes of the rally-prone Lendl and Seles never even won one.

For her part, Martina Navratilova won an extraordinary *nine* Wimbledons—and she seemed to appreciate the ninth one just as much as the first. 'They change it but it still feels the same,' the Czech-born American enthused, and there in a nutshell you have the tournament's appeal. While all four Slams are over a century old, Wimbledon is the only one that *looks* it. One of tennis's great traditions is droning on about Wimbledon's great traditions, and who am I to go and break with that now?

For a start, it's played on sacred turf: Wimbledon was where the game's rules were codified, and where its first tournament was played. It's because of the stadium's concentric layout that main courts all over the world are known as centre courts, even when they're not central at all.

And it's the only Slam still played on the sport's original surface. Tennis's proper name, lest we forget, is *lawn* tennis. It's not called 'clay tennis' or 'DecoTurf™ tennis'. Or 'Plexicushion™ tennis', come to that.

And the traditions certainly don't stop there. The other Slams use a complex computer system designed to verify line calls, called Hawk-Eye; Wimbledon has a hawk called Rufus to keep pesky pigeons away.

While other Slams call themselves 'championships', and use flat phrases like 'game, Federer', Wimbledon still offers Gentlemen's and Ladies' Singles titles, and refers to players as Mr or Miss. It's the only Slam without a skerrick of advertising, and has its very own livery, in purple and green.

In other Slams, spectators are able to book their tickets using newfangled devices like computers and phones. At Wimbledon, however, they queue. Generally for hours, often overnight, and *always* in an orderly fashion. The All England Club even has a lengthy code of conduct for 'The Queue'. 'You may not reserve a place in The Queue for somebody else,' it says, rather sadistically, 'other than in their short term absence.'

Of course, that's not the only code of conduct: Wimbledon has rules galore. One of the more famous requires that players wear white. While the other Slams contain all the colours of the rainbow (quite often, just in the one Nike shirt), Wimbledon's strict dress code demands 'no solid mass of colouring; little or no dark or bold colours; no fluorescent colours; preference towards pastel colours … and all other items of clothing including hats, socks and shoes to be almost entirely white.' And, when it comes to Club members, 'the dress standard for gentlemen is lounge suit or tailored jacket, shirt, tie, trousers and dress shoes. Ladies are expected to dress to a similar standard.'

And if they have any brains, they bring a raincoat as well. It's possible that there has been a Wimbledon that wasn't blighted by long, endless rain delays but if so, no-one can remember it.

You can't always be sure of seeing good tennis when you go to see Wimbledon, but low grey clouds come guaranteed. The worst rain delay famously came on 3 July 1996, when the singer Cliff Richard was sitting in the stands. Figuring that the crowd hadn't suffered enough during the hour-long halt to proceedings, he volunteered to entertain them some of his greatest 'hits', and kicked off with 'Singin' in the Rain'.

The Duke and Duchess of Kent were part of Sir Cliff's audience that day, and they're far from the first royals to have graced centre court. Wimbledon doesn't just attract the best tennis players, it attracts the best people as well. The Queen herself is an occasional visitor, and her father, George VI, actually entered the doubles in 1926 with a titled friend, only to be crushed in straight sets by a couple of commoners.

But we can be sure that George would have got a few quiet, genteel claps, however badly he might have played. Fortified by Pimms, champagne, and strawberries and cream, Wimbledon crowds will applaud just about anyone, provided they're well-behaved. 'New Yorkers love it when you spill your guts at the US Open,' says Jimmy Connors. 'Spill your guts at Wimbledon and they make you stop and clear it up.'

Wimbledon fast facts

Official name: The Championships
Governing body: Lawn Tennis Association
Founded: 1877
Current venue: The All England Lawn Tennis and Croquet Club, London
Surface: Grass
Held: From late June until early July
Trophies: Unnamed silver-gilt cup (men); The Venus Rosewater Dish (women)
Total prize money: £22,500,000
Average attendance: 490,000

Current singles champions: Novak Djokovic (Serbia); Petra Kvitová (Czech Republic)

Most singles titles: men

7	Roger Federer (Switzerland), William Renshaw (USA), Pete Sampras (USA)
5	Björn Borg (Sweden), Lawrence Doherty (UK)
4	Reginald Doherty (UK), Rod Laver (Australia), Anthony Wilding (NZ)
3	Wilfred Baddeley (UK), Boris Becker (Germany), Arthur Gore (UK), John McEnroe (USA), John Newcombe (Australia), Fred Perry (UK), Bill Tilden (USA)

Most singles titles: women

9	Martina Navratilova (USA)
8	Helen Wills (USA)
7	Dorothea Chambers (USA), Steffi Graf (Germany)
6	Lottie Dod (UK), Blanche Hillyard (UK), Billie Jean King (USA), Suzanne Lenglen (France), Venus Williams (USA), Helen Wills (USA)

Youngest singles title-winners

17	Boris Becker (Germany, 1985)
15	Lottie Dod (UK, 1887)

Oldest singles title-winners

41	Arthur Gore (UK, 1909)
38	Charlotte Cooper (UK, 1908)

Most consecutive singles titles

6	William Renshaw (1881–86)
6	Martina Navratilova (1982–87)

Strange but true: Over 1200 centre-court seats were destroyed by a Luftwaffe bomb in 1940. Fortunately, no-one was sitting in them at the time.

Wimbledon timeline

1858: The All England Croquet Club is launched at Worple Road in Wimbledon

1876: Lawn tennis is added to the club's activities

1877: The club organises a men's singles tournament to raise money for a new lawn roller, and draws up a code of rules for the event

1884: Ladies' singles and Gentlemen's doubles are added

1913: Ladies' doubles and mixed doubles are added

1915–18: Tournament cancelled due to World War I

1922: The tournament moves to its present site in Church Rd
The principal court retains the name 'Centre Court', despite the fact that it's placed to the side

1924: The seeding system is introduced

1930: Brame Hillyard becomes the first man to play in shorts

1936: Fred Perry takes out the title—the last Englishman to do so

1940: Several Centre Court seats are destroyed by bombing, and remain out of action for the next nine years

1940–45: Tournament cancelled due to World War II

1977: Virginia Wade takes out the title—the last Englishwoman to do so

1981: Mrs John Lloyd (or as we now know her, Chris Evert) becomes the last married woman to win the women's singles

1986: White balls are replaced by yellow ones because they are more visible to TV cameras

1987: A wooden racquet is used for the last time

2001: Goran Ivanisevic becomes the first and last wildcard to win the title (and also the only player whose name alternates consonants and vowels)

2009: A retractable roof is added to Centre Court

7/23102

The US Open

No-one likes talking in stereotypes, but when it comes to the US Open, there's really no choice. Whether the French Open is really as chic as its hosts like to say it is, or the Australian Open quite as g'day-mate friendly, the calendar's fourth Grand Slam is every bit as big, brash and boisterous as its venue, the biggest and loudest city in the States. New York, New York is a helluva town, and the US Open is a helluva tournament.

For a start, it's simply huge. 'Everything is large compared to the other Slams,' says world number 50 Varvara Lepchenko—'the giant city, the stadium, the people.' Flushing Meadows is far and away the biggest tennis venue in the world, with twenty outdoor courts and a centre court that seats 23,000, and no other tennis tournament sells more tickets. Over 700,000 spectators come to see the show every August, and, packed together, they can make quite a noise.

Sometimes called 'the city that never sleeps', New York is definitely the city that never shuts up. 'People in the crowd can really get pumped up,' says Pat Cash. 'They boo, they get involved.' They get up midpoint to wave hello to a neighbour, or climb over seats to buy hot dogs and beer. 'New York is a city full of energy and they bring it to the tennis.'

It's also a city full of air traffic: planes flying in and out of nearby La Guardia airport add the roar of powerful jet engines to the hoots, chants and cheers of the crowd. According to Pam Shriver, a player 'could close their eyes, and know in a second that they were in NYC just by the sound.'

And according to Sloane Stephens, they could know it by the saliva. The Florida-born rising star has been licked, hugged and chased by New York fans during the US Open, has had her ponytail pulled and has been hit by a racquet. 'I don't plan on going outside,' she said from her hotel room during the 2013 tournament, 'because I know that I will probably not make it out alive.'

And, as far as officials are concerned, this is mostly okay. The US Open is the *enfant terrible* of the tennis tour, a pesky, trashy Bart Simpson–type compared with Wimbledon's well-bred gent. 'We used to be very pernickety about spectators sitting down during play, but a few years ago, we began to take a more liberal view of what the fans can and cannot do,' says tournament director Michael Morrissey of the tournament's attitude to troublemakers, which is more or less 'Go right ahead'.

'It was less "Quiet please", because that sounded like we were treating them as naughty children. We were killing the energy. Now, I guess the issue is, "Are the players being disrupted by it?" If not, then we let it go.'

Need an example of disruption? Well, in 1977, they did once stop a John McEnroe match for a few minutes ... because a spectator had been shot in the leg. And a few games were also put on hold for a little while in the early eighties, when the fumes from locals burning their rubbish caused vocal protests from the crowd. And another game was stopped in 2010, because of a spectator brawl.

But even when play stops, there's plenty for fans to do. Pop songs blare out at changeovers, and giant video screens replay every point. On special nights, you might see Lenny Kravitz or Aretha bang out a few hits, or a troupe of Broadway showgirls sing on centre court.

Celebrity-spotting also helps pass the time, with the likes of Alec Baldwin, Jay-Z and Beyoncé all fairly regular guests. (And if all else fails, you'll still see Donald Trump.)

The overall effect is to 'make tennis show business,' says Serena Williams, who has four Flushing Meadows trophies in a cabinet at home. 'As a tennis player, when you walk out you have a feeling that cannot be duplicated anywhere.'

It's certainly a far cry from how things started out. The first US Open (or, rather, the first US National Championships) was held in 1881 at Newport, Rhode Island—a summer retreat straight out of a Ralph Lauren commercial, with its bright pink geraniums and long golden beaches, smart blue blazers and crisp white slacks. Players took the court to the sounds of classical music and flapping sails from nearby yachts. And you could be sure that no rubbish was ever burnt in Newport's gilded-age mansions. The Astors and Vanderbilts who lived in them would sooner have set fire to a servant.

That first tournament was won by Harvard student Richard Sears, and he went on to win seven more. US Opens have always seemed to suit US citizens. In the 133 years since the tournament was first staged in 1881, there have only six years in which an American player has not appeared in either the men's or women's singles final.

Perhaps only Americans can cope with Americans?

Anyway, I know I can't.

US Open fast facts

Official name: The US Open Tennis Championships

Governing body: The United States Tennis Association

Founded: 1881

Current venue: USTA Billie Jean King National Tennis Center, Flushing Meadows, New York

Surface: DecoTurf

Held: From late August until early September

Total prize money: $34,250,000

Average attendance: 700,000

Current singles champions: Marin Čilić (Croatia); Serena Williams (USA)

Most singles titles: men

7	William Larned (USA), Richard Sears (USA), Bill Tilden (USA)
5	Jimmy Connors (USA), Roger Federer (Switzerland), Pete Sampras (USA)
4	John McEnroe (USA), Robert Wrenn (USA)
3	Oliver Campbell (USA), Ivan Lendl (Czechoslovakia, USA), Fred Perry (UK), Malcolm Whitman (USA)

Most singles titles: women

8	Molla Mallory (Norway)
7	Helen Wills (USA)
6	Chris Evert (USA), Serena Williams (USA)
5	Margaret Court (Australia), Steffi Graf (Germany)
4	Pauline Betz Addie (USA), Maria Bueno (Brazil), Helen Jacobs (USA), Billie Jean King (USA), Alice Marble (USA), Elisabeth Moore (USA), Martina Navratilova (Czechoslovakia, USA), Hazel Hotchkiss Wightman (USA)

Youngest singles champions

19	Pete Sampras (USA, 1990)
16	Tracy Austin (USA, 1979)

Oldest singles champions

38	William Larned (USA, 1911)
42	Molla Mallory (Norway, 1926)

Most consecutive singles titles

7	Richard Sears (USA, 1881–87)
4	Helen Jacobs (USA, 1932–35), Molla Mallory (Norway, 1915–18)

Strange but true: The US Open has been played on all three surfaces at different times in its history: hardcourt, grass and clay.

US Open timeline

1881: Men's singles and doubles tournament held on the grass courts of Newport Casino, Rhode Island. Only members of the US National Lawn Tennis Association are permitted to enter

1887: Women's singles matches are added

1889: Women's doubles and mixed doubles are added

1915: The tournament is moved to the West Side Tennis Club at Forest Hills, New York

1924: The tournament is designated one of the four major tournaments by the ILTF

1968: The Open Era begins, and the American National Championships are renamed the US Open

1970: The US Open becomes the first Grand Slam to use tie breaks to decide a set that has reached 6–6

1973: The US Open becomes the first Grand Slam to award equal prize money to men and women

1975: The West Side Tennis Club switches from grass to clay, and adds floodlights, enabling night play for the first time in Grand Slam history

1977: A third-round match between John McEnroe and compatriot Eddie Dibbs is held up due to a shooting incident in the crowd

1978: The tournament moves to its present home at Flushing Meadows in Queens After winning on grass in 1974 and clay in 1976, Jimmy Connors takes out the first title at the new hardcourt venue, and becomes the only man to ever win the same Grand Slam on three different surfaces

1997: The $254 million Arthur Ashe Stadium opens, replacing the smaller, ailing Louis Armstrong Stadium as the primary venue for the tournament

2006: The Flushing Meadows complex is renamed in honour of four-time tournament champion and women's rights crusader Billie Jean King

The French Open

Wimbledon may be sacred turf, but Roland-Garros is sacred clay. The pinnacle of the clay court season—ten weeks or so of dogged Spanish baseliners battling it out from Monaco to Madrid—the French Open is defined by the mixture of rock, gravel and ground-up limestone which Parisians call *terre battue*.

Far and away the slowest surface in tennis—and one on which balls bounce relatively high—the red clay at Roland-Garros Stadium also makes it far and away the most demanding Grand Slam to play. Players win points by grinding out long rallies: by scampering around at breakneck speed and working their opponents from side to side. Powerful, big-serving players generally find their strengths neutralised, and players with poor concentration have no chance at all.

What this means is that the list of players who haven't won a French Open is, well, rather impressive. Pete Sampras, Boris Becker, John McEnroe, Stefan Edberg. Venus Williams, Maria Sharapova, Martina Hingis, Lindsay Davenport. Roger Federer has only ever managed to win one of them. And big-serving Andy Roddick never even made the Quarters.

Contrast this with a list of some recent Roland-Garros champs—Sergi Bruguera, Albert Costa, Gastón Guadio; Svetlana Kuznetsova, Francesca Schiavone, Anastasia Myskina—and you'll begin to see what I mean.

But the French Open is certainly not just for dogged triers. Champions whose game style is suited to the surface have found it a happy hunting ground indeed. Steffi Graf, Margaret Court and Chris Evert won a grand total of eight French Opens between them. Björn Borg won seven all by himself, and Rafael Nadal is currently on nine.

Which is not to say that the French crowds love him. 'There is only one set of supporters that is worse than the French and that is the Parisians,' Nadal's coach once told a radio station, after his Spanish protégé was jeered, booed and hissed at in the course of a five-set win. 'They say it themselves and it's true, the Parisian crowd is pretty stupid. I think the French don't like it when a Spaniard wins. Wanting someone to lose is a slightly conceited way of amusing yourself. They show the stupidity of people who think themselves superior.'

But if the French in fact like it when *any* foreigner wins, they do a good job keeping it to themselves. Roland-Garros crowds are notoriously bolshie. Players that French spectators have brought to tears in recent years include Martina Hingis and Serena Williams, while Maria Sharapova was once moved to scream at them, '*Allez* up your fucking arse!'

In their defence, however, they haven't had much to cheer at. While French players managed to take out the first thirty-five *Championnats de France*, this was because only French people were allowed to play. The tournament was an exclusively national event for its first three decades—a smallish affair, played at smallish suburban venues, and played only by members of French clubs. It wasn't until 1925 that the tournament became open to all and sundry, but the big development came two years later, when France's famous Four Musketeers managed to take out the Davis Cup on American soil, and set up a rematch in 1928.

Named for the 1920s movie *The Three Musketeers*, which broke box-office records, René Lacoste, Henri Cochet, Jacques Brugnon and Jean Borotra went on to dominate men's tennis during the late twenties and early thirties. But their first task was to defend their Davis Cup title. And half of Paris wanted to watch them at work.

The result was a glorious new stadium built to host this glorious sporting occasion (which the Musketeers very obligingly won). It was named after the original WWI flying ace, Roland Garros—and it's worth noting that the tournament is too. It's only us English-speakers who sit and watch the French Open. French people watch the *Tournoi de Roland-Garros*.

They don't really tend to win it, though. Since the Second World War, only three Frenchwomen (Nelly Adamson Landry, Françoise Dürr and Mary Pierce) have managed to take out the title, together with just two Frenchmen (Yannick Noah and Marcel Bernard).

'The problem with the French players, generally, is that they are very gifted, but not fighters,' says the tennis journalist Philippe Bouin. And an even bigger problem is that that's how Parisians like them. '[The reason] Spanish players have not really been appreciated by the French is not because they are Spaniards, but because they are fighters. The French crowd prefers attacking, gifted players. [In this country,] ambition is not a compliment. It's almost a bad word. "Ha, look, he's ambitious." So that's a very difficult situation for an athlete: as soon as you try to be ambitious, you have people mocking you.'

It is, he says, a mixed blessing. 'For instance, we would never have made the war in Iraq. But on the other hand, we may never win anything.'

French Open fast facts

Official name: Tournoi de Roland-Garros
Governing body: Fédération Française de Tennis
Founded: 1891
Current venue: Stade Roland-Garros, Paris
Surface: Clay
Held: From late May until early June
Trophies: Coupe des Mousquetaires (men); Coupe Suzanne Lenglen (women)
Total prize money: €25,000,000
Average attendance: 420,000

Current singles champions: Rafael Nadal (Spain); Maria Sharapova (Russia)

Most singles titles: men

9	Rafael Nadal (Spain)
8	Max Decugis (France)
6	Björn Borg (Sweden)
5	Henri Cochet (France)
4	Paul Aymé (France), André Vacherot (France)
3	Maurice Germot (France), Gustavo Kuerten (Brazil), René Lacoste (France), Ivan Lendl (Czechoslovakia, USA), Mats Wilander (Sweden)

Most singles titles: women

7	Chris Evert (USA)
6	Steffi Graf (Germany), Suzanne Lenglen (France)
5	Margaret Court (Australia), Françoise Masson (France)
4	Kate Gillou (France), Justine Henin (Belgium), Jeanne Matthey (France), Helen Wills (USA)

Youngest singles champions

17	Michael Chang (USA, 1989)
16	Monica Seles (Serbia, 1990)

Oldest singles champions

34	Andrés Gimeno (Spain, 1972)
33	Zsuzsa Körmöczy (Hungary, 1958)

Most consecutive singles titles

8	Rafael Nadal (Spain, 2005–09, 2010–2014)
4	Suzanne Lenglen (France, 1920–23), Jeanne Matthey (France, 1909–12)

Strange but true: At 33 acres, Roland-Garros is less than half the size of the other current Grand Slam venues.

French Open timeline

1891: The International Championships of Tennis is held at the Île de Puteaux, a small club on the western outskirts of Paris—one of four alternating venues over the next four decades

Despite the name, the tournament is limited to members of French clubs

1897: Women's singles matches are added

1902: Mixed doubles are added

1907: Women's doubles are added

1915–19: Tournament cancelled due to World War I

1925: The tournament became open to amateurs from all over the world and is designated a major championship by the ILTF

1927: The Four Musketeers (Jacques 'Toto' Brugnon, Jean Borotra, Henri Cochet and René Lacoste) unexpectedly win the Davis Cup on American soil, and thus set up a rematch to take place in Paris the next year

1928: Roland-Garros Stadium is built to house the Davis Cup final, and becomes the new home of the Championships

1933: Jack Crawford became the first non-French player to win at Roland-Garros

1940–1945: Tournament cancelled due to World War II

1956: Althea Gibson becomes the first African-American player to win a Grand Slam event

1968: Roland-Garros opens the Open Era and becomes the first Grand Slam to welcome pros

1983: Yannick Noah takes out the title—the last Frenchman to do so

2007: The tournament becomes the last Grand Slam to award equal prize money to men and women

2011: Li Na becomes the first Chinese national to win a Grand Slam

2012: Rafael Nadal beats Novak Djokovic to win his seventh French Open title, setting a new record

2014: After a lengthy legal squabble, in which a move away from Roland-Garros was canvassed, plans get underway to expand the size of the venue by 60 per cent

The Australian Open

While the Australian Open is the least prestigious Grand Slam, it would very likely be most players' favourite. 'It's kind of like the "Happy Slam",' says four-time champ Roger Federer. 'You get here and are happy to play again.'

Often described as world's best tournament—not least, by the people who run it—the Melbourne major comes hot on the heels of the Christmas holidays and sees all the players fit, fresh and raring to go. Sunny weather, friendly fans, massive prize money and an inner-city location all help the cause, as do some fantastic facilities. Armed, as they are, with ample government support, tournament organisers bend over backwards to cater to players' needs, and then jump through a series of hoops.

'I like everything here,' gushes Novak Djokovic. 'The Central Court, the surface, the playing conditions, and especially the incredible atmosphere in the stands. This is the most colourful Grand Slam, with fans from Serbia, Sweden, Croatia, Greece ... It certainly has a very special flavour.'

'I feel like this tournament definitely has the best facilities out of any of the majors,' agrees Venus Williams. '[It's] constantly improving.'

And the tennis isn't too bad either. For a start, the Australian Open generally sees players at their physical peak. The French Open comes at the end of the long, grinding clay court season, the US towards the end of the year. Wimbledon is played on a surface which takes time to master—and begins just two weeks after the French Open. The Australian Open's hardcourt, on the other hand, caters to a variety of playing styles (though in recent years, some have said it's too slow).

Plenty of people have also said it's too hot. Played right in the middle of the Australian summer—the season of bush-fires, dust and drought—it's the only Grand Slam with its own extreme heat policy, which allows umpires to suspend play during a stinker.

They probably should have suspended it during the 2007 Australian Open, a fortnight which saw on-court temperatures soar above 40 degrees. That tournament saw Caroline Wozniacki's plastic water bottle melt on court and Jo-Wilfried Tsonga's shoes soften in the heat. Several players had to rehydrate with an intravenous drip, and Jelena Janković burnt her bum on an uncovered seat. But the highlight came from Canadian world number 122, Frank Dancevic, who collapsed to the ground unconscious during his first-round match—and even managed to hallucinate, too. 'I was dizzy from the middle of the first set and then I saw Snoopy and I thought, "Wow Snoopy, that's weird",' Dancevic said. 'I couldn't keep my balance anymore and I leaned over the fence and when I woke up people were all around me.'

'It's hazardous to be out there, it's dangerous. Until somebody dies, they're going to keep playing playing matches in this heat ... and personally I don't think it's fair.'

Whether or not the tournament is fair, most players agree that it's *far*. Australia's geographic remoteness meant that very few foreign players entered The Australasian Championships in the early twentieth century, when the trip from Europe by ship took around forty days. Superstars like Bill Tilden, Henri Cochet and René Lacoste never made the journey, and most ordinary players didn't make enough to even contemplate it.

While the advent of air travel helped to alleviate this problem, the southern hemisphere Slam was still grand in name only throughout the fifties, sixties and seventies, thanks to poor prize money, idiotic scheduling over Christmas and New Year, and a habit of shifting venue from city to city, however crap a city's stadium might happen to be.

Björn Borg only bothered to come to Australia once during his career, and Ilie Năstase made his first and last trip at age thirty-five. So the Australian Open's winners tended to be players like Johan Kriek, Brian Teacher and Christine O'Neil. Lovely people, probably, but if they're tennis superstars then, goddammit, so am I.

The nadir came in 1970, when even *Australian* stars like Rod Laver, Ken Rosewall and Roy Emerson found that they had prior engagements elsewhere.

But come 1988, things were looking up. It was the year of the Australian bicentenary that Tennis Australia was given a big, fat wad of cash, and a big, fat mandate to change whatever it liked. The idiotic scheduling was the first thing to go: Australian Opens are now held in late January, rather than over Christmas. And it was also goodbye to run-down wooden stadiums, and old-fashioned (and sometimes poorly mowed) grass.

In their place, spectators said hello to Melbourne Park, a brand-new, gazillion-dollar complex with a whiz-bang retractable roof. Over 266,000 tennis fans went through the turnstiles that year—an increase of 90 per cent on 1987—and Australian Opens these days tend to get almost thrice that, making it the world's best-attended tournament after the US Open.

Unfortunately for the Johan Krieks, Brian Teachers and Christine O'Neils of the world, this means that all the best players have started attending as well.

Australian Open fast facts

Official name: The Australian Open Tennis Championships

Governing body: Tennis Australia

Founded: 1905

Current venue: Melbourne Park, Melbourne

Surface: Plexicushion

Held: From late January until early February

Trophies: The Norman Brookes Challenge Cup (men);
The Daphne Akhurst Memorial Cup (women)

Total prize money: $30,000,000

Average crowd numbers: 650,000

Current singles champions: Stan Wawrinka (Switzerland); Li Na (China)

Most singles titles: men

6	Roy Emerson (Australia)
4	Andre Agassi (USA), Jack Crawford (Australia), Novak Djokovic (Serbia), Roger Federer (Switzerland), Ken Rosewall (Australia)
3	James Anderson (Australia), Rod Laver (Australia), Adrian Quist (Australia), Mats Wilander (Switzerland)
2	Boris Becker (Germany), John Bromwich (Australia), Ashley Cooper (Australia), Jim Courier (USA), Stefan Edberg (Sweden), Rodney Heath (Australia), Ivan Lendl (Czechoslovakia, USA), John Newcombe (Australia), Frank Sedgman (Australia), Guillermo Vilas (Argentina), Anthony Wilding (New Zealand), Pat Wood (Australia)

Most singles titles: women

11	Margaret Court (Australia)
6	Nancye Bolton (Australia)
5	Daphne Cozens (Australia), Serena Williams (USA)
4	Evonne Goolagong (Australia), Steffi Graf (Germany), Monica Seles (Yugoslavia)

Youngest singles champions

18	Ken Rosewall (Australia, 1953)
16	Martina Hingis (Switzerland, 1997)

Oldest singles champions

37	Ken Rosewall (Australia, 1972)
35	Thelma Long (Australia, 1954)

Most consecutive singles titles

5	Roy Emerson (Australia, 1963–1967)
7	Margaret Court (Australia, 1960–1966)

Strange but true: In 1906 and 1912, the Australian Open was played in New Zealand.

Australian Open timeline

1905: The Australasian Championships are played at the Warehouseman's Cricket Ground in St Kilda Road, Melbourne—the first of many grass-court venues on both sides of the Tasman Sea

1923: The International Lawn Tennis Federation designates the tournament a major championship

1927: The tournament's name is changed to the Australian Championships—no more New Zealand

1946: The US Davis Cup team are the first foreign players to arrive by aircraft

1969: The tournament becomes open to amateurs and professionals (a year after the other Grand Slams) and changes its name to the Australian Open

1971: Kooyong Lawn Tennis Club in Melbourne becomes the tournament's permanent home—no more shifting cities from year to year

1976: Mark Edmondson wins the men's singles—the last Australian man to do so

1977: The tournament shifts from January to December, with the result that two tournaments are held

1978: Chris O'Neil wins the women's singles—the last Australian woman to do so

1987: The tournament shifts back to January, and is held at Kooyong's grass courts for the final time

1988: The tournament moves to Melbourne Park, with its Rebound Ace surface and retractable roof, and records a 90 per cent increase on the previous year's attendance

2003: The tournament begins billing itself as the Grand Slam of Asia–Pacific

2007: On-court temperatures reach 40 degrees Celsius
Hawk-Eye system is introduced as back-up to human line umpires
Two-dozen policemen are needed to control a brawl between 150 Serb and Croat fans

2008: Rebound Ace surface is abandoned in favour of the faster acrylic blue Plexicushion

2013: Australian Open voted the world's best tennis tournament in *Tennis Magazine*

- 3 -
THE TOUR

So, how many professional tennis players are there, exactly? I have spent many hours trying to find the answer to this question, and the best I can give you is 'rather a lot'.

The ATP rankings system lists the top 2200 male players every week, while the WTA supplies the top 2000 women, but both systems exclude all the not-so-successful-but-still-very-much-professional players who are trying their darndest to get on the list. From fading journeymen to rising child prodigies and one-time college stars who aren't as good as they think, the tennis world is full of part-time professionals: sad-faced types plugging away at obscure suburban tournaments, and wishing that their prize money could cover the cost of the flight. There's no point trying to keep track of them all. That's a job for debt collectors.

Here, then, are some of the players, on-court and off, to look out for, next time you switch on a Grand Slam. It's by no means an exhaustive list—but, believe me, that's not what you want.

Identikit baseliners

Serve, forehand, backhand, winner.

Serve, backhand, error.

Serve, yawn, snore.

Many people say that we're living in a golden age of tennis—and as far as standards go, they could well be right. The world might never see a better woman player than Serena Williams. And the 'big four' players in men's tennis—Novak Djokovic, Rafael Nadal, Roger Federer and Andy Murray—are all among the biggest talents to have played the game.

However, there exists a different view. Broadly speaking, it's 'today's tennis sucks'. Once upon a time, the best tennis showcased all sorts of styles—from speedy counterpunching to kamikaze serve-volleying, artful drop shots and attacking lobs—but today's pros all play the same way. They all stay on the baseline and hit hard topspin groundstrokes until at some point someone makes a mistake. It's a bit like watching a metronome, only not quite as interesting or fun.

'I don't think it's ever coming back, I really don't,' says Pete Sampras of the serve-and-volley technique, which not all that long ago gave him fourteen Grand Slams. 'It's difficult to learn to do, and it's hard to be successful with it at first, and kids and coaches don't like failure ... [So now] everyone is staying back and hitting the crap out of the ball ... [There just happens to be] four or five guys that are a lot better at it than the rest.'

Of course, tennis has always had people who played this way: Borg, Lendl and Agassi all spring to mind. But those guys had McEnroe, Becker and Sampras on the other side of the net—or rather, *at the net*, volleying their groundstrokes away. The best tennis spectacles often involve a clash of techniques, and once upon a time, fans saw them in spades.

The 2002 Wimbledon final is often seen as the day that the serve-volley died. That game between Lleyton Hewitt and David Nalbandian represented the first time since 1978 that two baseliners had slugged it out for the grass-court title—a state of affairs which has since become the norm. If at first you don't succeed, then whack, whack again.

'All of a sudden [after that final], the game became a baseline game,' says John McEnroe. 'I would have bet everything, my house, that you would never see that type of tennis in the men's game where all the players are staying back. I would have lost my house. I think ideally the best tennis is when you have two different styles going at it. People enjoy that more.'

But it would be wrong to blame Hewitt and Nalbandian. They were just accessories to the crime. Variable tennis's real killer has been modern technology: modern racquets, modern courts, modern balls. Today's players can hit deep, looping groundstrokes more or less at will, and they can hit them harder than ever before.

As Taylor Dent, one of the last serve-volleyers, once explained, returners can now 'get so much dip on the ball. In the past, if you were serving and volleying, it was really tough for the guy to get a return down at your feet because you can't generate that kind of spin off a first serve. Generally speaking, you're just trying to keep it low over the net. But now, if you don't really stretch a guy out, it's coming back at your feet, and then they can hit passing shots so hard because they can generate so much spin … The main reason you don't see more serve and volley is because it's too much of an advantage to give away [playing that style].'

The modern player is basically a power athlete. And some modern spectators are becoming powerfully bored.

Big grunters

The late, great Peter Ustinov once attended a match featuring the still-alive and great Monica Seles. A few games and about six million 'aaarghs', 'eeeeeks' and 'ooooohs' into the contest, he turned to a friend and calmly commented, 'I'd hate to be in the hotel room next door on her wedding night.'

You'd be able to hear many of today's champions on the next *floor*. While not many other tennis players adopted her two-handed forehand, and Seles thankfully remains the only player to have been brutally stabbed, her habit of shrieking and grunting has become de rigueur in the women's game.

Serena Williams and Victoria Azarenka are both enthusiastic grunters, while the banshee-like Maria Sharapova once clocked a screech of 101 decibels on the grunt-o-meter—a volume not too far from a lion's roar. 'I've done this ever since I started playing tennis and I'm not going to change,' says the willowy Russian, who has even been known to shriek while hitting a slice.

But Sharapova is as quiet as a mouse compared to Michelle Larcher de Brito. The rising Portuguese star has the volume and vocal range of an opera singer holding a megaphone, while using a chainsaw and driving a truck. Brito's best effort on record is 109 decibels. Her best unrecorded effort would make a grown man weep.

'Nobody can tell me to stop grunting,' she said during the 2009 French Open, after a lot of people told her to stop grunting because it was distracting opponents and annoying the fans. 'Tennis is an individual sport and I'm an individual player. If they have to fine me, go ahead, because I'd rather get fined than lose a match because I had to stop grunting. If it has inconvenienced the other player, there's nothing I can really do about it, because I don't really want to change anything ... I'm here to win. That's it. If people don't like my grunting they can always leave.'

It's worth noting that Brito is a product of the same Florida tennis academy that gave the world Serena, Sharapova and Seles. Could grunting actually be on its syllabus? There's certainly a theory going around that using your voice box is a neat way to efficiently trap and release air, and thus bring on a nice, deep breath before your next shot.

Another theory is that this is crap.

But whatever grunting's physical benefits may or may not be, the *perception* of a benefit may be helpful enough. 'The timing of when they actually grunt helps them with the rhythm of how they're hitting and how they're pacing things,' sports psychologist Louise Deeley says of today's tennis banshees. 'It may be that their perception is that if they grunt, they are hitting it harder. It's going to give you confidence and a sense of being in control of your game.'

They may not be in control for too much longer. In recent years, fans, TV broadcasters and top players like Caroline Wozniacki have all spoken out against shrieking out, and the

WTA reportedly has plans to start arming umpires with devices that will help them to measure noise levels on court.

For the likes of Martina Navratilova, this is good news. She argues that grunting does nothing to help the grunter ('Roger Federer doesn't make a noise when he hits the ball—go and listen') and a great deal to distract their opponents. 'The grunting has reached an unacceptable level. It is cheating, pure and simple. It is time for something to be done.'

Until then, I suggest you wear earplugs.

Obsessive-compulsives

'I do not have superstitions,' says Novak Djokovic—a man who, during a Grand Slam, will never use the same shower twice in a row. 'I have *routines*. I call them routines.'

Watch closely and you'll find that rather a few players are prone to 'routines': little quirks, tics, habits and rituals that they keep repeating again and again. The Djoker, for example, also likes to bounce the ball a lot before every serve—and by 'a lot', I mean up to twenty-five times.

'You're looking to recreate your good performances,' says two-time US Open winner Tracy Austin, and that can involve trying to recreate the particular circumstance in which a performance took place. 'Players are seeking consistency in a world of unknowns. There's so much you can't control, the score keeps ticking away, the match has a lot of moving parts, and there is nobody there to calm you down. So if there is any one thing you can control, it brings you comfort, and that comfort gives you confidence.'

Some players' routines can be seen from the moment they step on court. The likes of Ana Ivanovic, Justine Henin and Maria Sharapova literally go out of their way to not step on a line.

Another Sharapova tic involves hair. Like Ivan Lendl (a man who would use his racquet to remove clay from the soles of his shoes … even if he was playing on hardcourt), the Russian likes to tuck her fringe behind her ear—even if it already is. 'If you tell her she can't do it, she might not play as well,' says sports psychologist Jim Loehr. 'You would have to redo the whole readying response, getting that balance and chemistry right.'

One of Björn Borg's routines also involved hair. He liked to start every Wimbledon completely clean-shaven and then not go near a razor for the next two weeks. The technique helped net him five trophies, but it doesn't seem to have done quite as much for the career of another player. Jerzy Janowicz will only ever shave after a loss. Which, as it happens, means he shaves quite a lot.

It seems safe to assume that Heather Watson never shaves her face, what with her being a woman and all that, but that doesn't mean she's devoid of routines. The British world number 92 wears the same dress every day during a major—a habit that was once shared by Sam Stosur. 'I stopped being superstitious in 2009 after the [French Open],' says Stosur. 'For the whole tournament [she reached the semifinals], I wore the same dress, the same socks, the same hat—it drove me crazy. Every night, I had to put it all in the wash. Everything had to be the same, even my hair. It was enough to drive you around the bend, so I stopped and now I don't have any superstitions.'

If only Serena Williams could say the same thing. A woman who will always bounce the ball five times before hitting her first serve, and twice before hitting her second, Serena wears the same pair of socks throughout every Grand Slam. She is also fond of always using the same shower, and of wearing the same pair of shower sandals.

Not, perhaps, the most hygienic of habits—but Andre Agassi is in no position to criticise. The Las Vegas showman played without underpants during the second half of his career. The habit started by accident at the 1999 French Open, when he was forced to free-ball, but got away with a win. 'I got to the locker room and realised I'd forgotten my underwear. What can a man do? I just commando-ed it. After that it was a case of "If it ain't broke, don't fix it." It actually feels good.'

But while Andre was laissez faire when it came to his testicles, he liked his ball *kids* to stay firmly in place. The American would often refuse to begin a point if one of them was positioned even slightly off-centre, or was squatting too far to the left or the right.

Ball kids also did it tough at matches involving Richard Gasquet, Goran Ivanisevic and Conchita Martínez. All three players would insist on serving with the same ball with which they last won a service point, however much time and inconvenience it took to find it.

But at least they never tried to *smell* the balls, like Dominika Cibulková. 'It's ... what I do on the court when I have new balls,' she explained at the 2012 French Open. 'I just smell them. It's maybe also for the luck. I do it all my life.'

We can only hope that Goran Ivanisevic doesn't plan to watch the *Teletubbies* all his life, but he famously did so every morning during one Wimbledon tournament. And every night saw him sit at the same table of the same restaurant, and eat exactly the same entree and main course and dessert. Didn't he realise that these rituals never work, an interviewer later asked him. 'I didn't,' replied the Croatian. 'Because it worked. I won Wimbledon.'

But if obsessive attention to ritual is the secret of Rafael Nadal's success, I think that we're all better off being failures. As neatly summarised by Will Swanton in *The Australian* newspaper, Nadal's pre-match checklist of 'must-dos' is quite simply OCD.

▸ He must have a cold shower 45 minutes before a match.
▸ He must carry one racquet on to the court.
▸ He must have five other racquets in his bag.
▸ He must have wrapped his own white grip on his racquets in the locker room.

- His bag must be placed next to his chair, on a towel, never on the chair.
- He must sprint to the baseline after the spin of the coin. A split-step and then a jog around the back court.
- He must towel down between every point. It can be ace or double-fault—he must towel down as if he's covered in sweat.
- He must run his hair behind both ears.
- He must touch his nose.
- He must pick at his underpants.
- He must drink from two water bottles at changeovers. One bottle has cold water, one is warm.
- He must face the labels of his drink bottles to the end he is about to play from.
- He must never rise from his seat before his opponent.
- He must wait at the net post so his opponent can reach his seat first.
- He must never walk on the sidelines as if he is avoiding cracks in the pavement.
- On clay, he must run his foot along the plastic baseline on the side of the court he is about to play from.
- At the Australian Open, when going from one side of the court to the other, he must walk across the *MELBOURNE* sign.

Poor bastard.

Cyborgs

The human face has forty-three muscles, from the buccinator to the corrugator supercilii—not to mention everyone's favourite, the temporoparietalis. (And who could forget the levaltor labbii suserioris alaeque nasi muscle? It has such a snappy name, after all.)

In combination, these muscles can create an almost infinite number of facial expressions ... provided that you're not a tennis player. Most of those guys only seem to have one.

The tennisbot trend may have started with Björn Borg and Chris Evert, two highly successful players who had about as much personality as a small piece of lettuce. Called Ice Borg and the Ice Maiden by their adoring fans, and 'a great advertisement for football' by everyone else, both players stuck with the one facial expression throughout every single moment of their careers, regardless of what was happening in a match. If they hit a great winner, they'd look grim and determined. If they made a crucial error, they'd look determined and grim.

When Evert and Borg powered down in the early eighties, another cyborg-like baseliner began to boot up. A man not devoid of personality off the court—according to Andre Agassi, he liked to 'sit around the locker room completely naked with just his shoes on, telling jokes all day'—Ivan Lendl was like a poker player on the court, his face never revealing anything beyond a desire to get on with the match. 'I wanted him to become a machine, to hide his feelings, to wear an unemotional mask,' says the Czech-born player's childhood coach, Wojtek Fibak, and you'd have to say: mission accomplished!

Since Lendl's era, tennis has had all sorts of cyborgs—and they've started to take their 'game face' to the press room as well. While an interview with Jimmy Connors or John McEnroe could be an all-day quote-athon, complete with boasts, gags and critiques of rivals, today's tennis interviews are diplomatic, polished and classy affairs. In other words, totally dull.

But perhaps their 'game face' is their *real* face? Could it be that some modern players are simply dull? It's certainly true that the demands of today's game are so all-consuming that they wouldn't leave much for an actual life. Take this recent Q&A with Aussie ace Sam Stosur.

Q: What is the first thing you do after a match?
A: Go to the gym.
Q: What was your craziest night on the tour?

A: I don't really have crazy nights or go out late, so I don't know what to say.

Q: What is your most stupid nickname?

A: Generally I get called 'Sam' or 'Sammy'.

Food for thought, perhaps, but Latvian star Ernests Gulbis thinks something else. The Latvian player blames the 'big four'. 'I respect Roger [Federer], Rafa [Nadal], Novak [Djokovic] and [Andy] Murray but, for me, all four of them are boring players,' he told the French newspaper, *L'Equipe.*

> Their interviews are boring. Honestly, they are crap. I often go on YouTube to watch the interviews. With tennis, I quickly stop. It is a joke. It is Federer who started this fashion. He has a superb image of the perfect Swiss gentleman. I repeat, I respect Federer but I don't like it that young players try to imitate him. When I hear them answer like Roger, I am terrified by phrases like: 'I had a little bit more success at certain moments and that is how I won' ... I would like interviews to be more like in boxing. OK, maybe those guys are not the most brilliant on earth but, when they face each other down at the weigh-in, they bring what the fans want: war, blood, emotion. All that is missing in tennis, where everything is clean and white with polite handshakes and some nice shots, while the people want to see broken racquets and hear outbursts on the court.

> Novak Djokovic was recently asked about Gulbis's accusation that he was, well, boring. And he gave an answer that was, well, boring. 'I haven't heard about his comments, and I haven't talked with him about that, but everybody has their own opinion, so that's difficult to judge something or somebody,' he said. 'We have certain rules and ways that our tennis is functioning in our sport, and that you have to respect. I try to look at it on a positive side. I think that especially the top players are very

respectful toward the sport and toward, you know, people who are appreciating and following the sport, to the media, and also to each other. This is very important. Even though it's individual sport, we still have very respectful and healthy relationships. It sends a good message out there.'

Yeah … I guess you're right. Thanks, Novak.

Yawn.

Child prodigies

Every parent thinks that their child is special—and, when it comes to tennis, some of them are right.

Tennis is the sport of child prodigies—of skinny little kids in big white shorts neglecting their schoolwork so they can receive state-of-the-art training and make millions instead. Europe and the USA are full of expensive and exclusive tennis academies trying to find the next Roger Federer—or, at least, trying to humour parents so they will keep sending cheques.

'Coming here was my father's idea,' said seventeen-year-old Eddie Schwartz of the Palmer Academy in Florida. 'I had to do some adjusting, get my grades up. At some of the other places the kids can get away with not going to school, but here it's "no this, no that"—curfews, random drug testing. I used to play an hour a day, now I'm on the court four or five hours.'

Eddie said this to the *New York Times* in 1992. And his name hasn't featured in a newspaper since.

For every Michael Chang (winner of the French Open at age seventeen) and Maureen Connolly (nine Slams by nineteen) there are tens of thousands of Eddie Schwartz types who never quite made it onto the tour.

And there are also plenty of prodigies who *did* become professional, but then didn't do very much. Some of them are cut down by injury, like Andrea Jaeger, who was world number two in 1985, until a shoulder injury ended her career two years later.

And others were maybe never that good. Take Michigan-born Aaron Krickstein, who barely lost a match as a junior, and then became the youngest-ever player to make the top twenty at the very tender age of sixteen. Greatness seemed certain. But greatness never came. Krickstein finished his career with a workmanlike 395–256 record and now makes a buck selling saltwater aquariums.

Or take Russian-born beauty Anna Kournikova, who remains one of the most Googled athletes on the face of the earth. The world junior champion at fourteen (and the youngest-ever player to win the Orange Bowl), she burst onto the pro tour in a blaze of publicity, and was a Wimbledon semifinalist by the age of sixteen. 'Anna is a shot maker,' said the world's most famous tennis coach, Nick Bolletieri, who helped engineer Kournikova's first multi-million management deal. Which she signed at age nine. 'She has the ability to create situations on the court that very few people can create. And at the net she's brilliant. She hits volleys from all angles. The only person I could compare her to is John McEnroe.'

Well, possibly, Nick. But John McEnroe *did* win seventy-seven singles titles. At the time she announced her retirement from tennis, Kournikova had managed to win a combined total of none.

But for all Kournikova's looks, glamour and superstar boyfriends (well, okay: dyed blonde hair, *Maxim* covers and Enrique Iglesias), she's a lot less interesting than Jennifer Capriati, the most famous fallen prodigy of all. Even though she managed to pick herself up and win Slams in her mid-twenties, Capriati's first Grand Slam title in 2001 came no less than eleven years after her debut as a fourteen-year-old, when she quickly became the youngest person to be ranked in the top ten. Eleven years in which she contemplated suicide. Eleven years in which she was charged with shoplifting and spent time in rehab. Eleven years in which she repeatedly broke down in tears. 'I really was not happy with myself, my tennis, my life, my parents, my coaches, my friends,' Capriati has since said of that time. 'When I looked in the mirror, I actually saw this distorted image: I was so ugly and fat, I just wanted to kill myself really.'

And even after she'd turned her tennis around, her spirits remained pretty low: 'I was on top of the world, but something was still missing inside.' Since her retirement, Capriati has been rushed to hospital due to a suspected suicide attempt, and charged with battery and stalking.

All in all, not such a good life. Parents of future 'prodigies' might want to take note.

Anonymous Eastern Europeans

What do get when you mix a Cibulková with a Makarova, then throw in a Pavlyuchenkova and a Rybáriková and a Hlaváčková? The answer, of course, is the WTA Tour—a spectacle rich in earnest baseliners from Bratislava and athletic grunters from lower Gdańsk.

Twas not always thus. During the seventies and eighties, the women's tour was all about Americans, and things weren't too different once the Berlin Wall went down. In 1990, only six of the top fifty women came from Eastern Europe. In 2000, the number was nine.

Today, however, there are seven Eastern European women in the top ten, and a further thirty-two to round out the top 100. Agnieszka Radwańska will be the world's number one player pretty soon, so long as Tsvetana Pironkova doesn't get there first.

Of course, this is a wonderful story—a triumph of pluck, grit and determination. (And perestroika. And quite possibly glasnost). But it can also be a bit difficult to keep track of who's who. 'With our long names, it can be hard to put the face with the name,' concedes 2010 Wimbledon finalist Vera Zvonareva.

'They ask you as you sign an autograph, "What is your name?"' says Vera's fellow Russian, Elena Vesnina, of the many devoted tennis fans she sees in the West.

The main reason for the Eastern European identity crisis (apart from the fact that these people don't really do vowels) is that their success is so very cyclical. Every season seems to see a new batch of stars emerge from behind the old Iron Curtain—and by the time you've mastered their names, they've turned totally crap.

Want examples? Well, Jelena Janković and Dinara Safina both enjoyed brief spells at number one without ever winning a Grand Slam, while Anastasia Myskina and Ana Ivanovic managed to win one major each without ever winning much else. Petra Kvitová and Svetlana Kuznetsova, on the other hand, have managed to snare *two* Slams each. But could you pick either of them out of a police line-up?

But all that could be set to change. With the all-conquering Belgians now safely retired, and the Williams sisters likely to follow suit in the next couple of years, the current batch of Eastern Europeans may just be set for a long stay at the top. Will Ekaterina Makarova grace tomorrow's magazine covers? Will Anastasia Sergeyevna Pavlyuchenkova soon be a household name?

If so, we better start practising it now.

Brash Americans

Tennis players are expected to keep their emotions to themselves. Americans, on the other hand, are not. Call them brash or call them entertaining (or be balanced, and call them both), Americans have added plenty of colour over the years to a game that likes its players to wear white.

The first American iconoclast (or egoist, if that's the term you prefer) was the 1920s star Big Bill Tilden. 'Tennis is more than just a sport,' Bill was wont to declare. 'It's an art, like the ballet, or like a performance in the theater. When I step on court I see the footlights in front of me. I hear the whispering of the audience. I feel an icy shudder.'

So do I, Bill, so do I.

This theatrical impulse sometimes caused Tilden to deliberately drop sets, so he could oh-so-dramatically start to fight his way back. And in later life it caused him to lose all his money, by investing in bad Broadway plays. But it was in his constant clashes with officialdom that Big Bill tended to put on his finest performances: he wasn't so much a prima donna as a total prick. One of Tilden's many spats was with the All England Club, which at the time expected all its singles players to sign up for mixed doubles as well. 'Women emasculate genius,' he said by way of refusal. 'They have ploys and they make petty demands of their partners.'

Not, perhaps, the most reasonable viewpoint—but Bobby Riggs would have probably approved. The world's best player in the late 1940s, Riggs is now best remembered for coming out of retirement in the 1970s to challenge the world's best woman to a tennis match. He would, he said, 'put Billie Jean King and all the other Women's Libbers back where they belong—in the kitchen and the bedroom'; the weaker sex had no place in professional sport. Over 55 million TV viewers watched Riggs arrive at Houston stadium in a big golden rickshaw pulled by six busty models ... and then proceed to lose in straight sets.

Unlike Big Bill Tilden, however, Riggs kept an open mind when it came to his doubles partners. Over the years, they included a donkey, an elephant and a lion cub. He was a man who would do absolutely anything for attention, and then try to do it again.

But to his credit, Riggs never played with John McEnroe—that would be too tacky even for him. The 1970s were a high point for American 'individualism', with the likes of Arthur Ashe and Billie Jean King helping to reshape the pro tour, and the likes of Jimmy Connors being shamelessly crass. But Superbrat was the biggest 'individual' of all, and it was at Wimbledon that he did his best work. In that small, seemingly harmless London suburb, poor McEnroe encountered 'vultures' and 'trash' and 'liars' and 'cheats'. He was persecuted by 'incompetent fools' and 'disgraces to mankind' and four different officials who had set out to 'screw' him. 'This place stinks, it reeks,' Superbrat was once heard to bellow. It really was 'the pits of the world'.

'I've never seen Wimbledon so mad, I mean burning,' said Ashe, of the All England Club's reaction to that most memorable of Wimbledon debuts. 'Not even when Connors insulted the Queen by not showing up for the centenary celebration in 1977.' Not to be outdone, Mac then did some not-showing-up of his own, boycotting the traditional black-tie winners dinner when he finally won the trophy in 1980. 'I wanted to spend [the night] with my family and friends and the people who had supported me,' he explained a few days later, 'not a bunch of stiffs who were 70–80 years old, telling you that you're acting like a jerk.'

For many years, another large American personality chose to boycott Wimbledon altogether, not liking the stuffy atmosphere and super-strict dress code. With his two-tone mullet and stonewashed denim shorts, and dangly earring and tight, pink, stretch pants, Andre Agassi saw himself as 'the ultimate showman'. 'Image is everything,' he proclaimed in a Nike commercial. If it is, he's in serious trouble.

In the past ten years, the standard of American tennis has declined, and the standard of American showmanship has, alas, declined with it. But we do, at least, still have Serena: friend of Paris Hilton and Kim Kardashian, and the buxom owner of a T-shirt with the slogan 'Are you looking at my titles?' As long as tennis has someone who's prepared to wear bright pink catsuits, it will always be a colourful sport.

Battling Brits

Wimbledon may be held at the All England Club, but its list of male trophy-winners is anything but. In the almost eight decades since Manchester's Fred Perry took home the trophy, it's been held by seventeen Americans and nine Australians. And two Germans and two Spaniards and two Swedes. A Frenchman and a Serbian have both had some time in the sun, and so has a Dutchman —and a Croatian and a Czech. Even Egyptians have won more Wimbledons than Englishmen in the seventy-seven years since Fred's fateful win.

Then along came Andy Murray. Not, perhaps, the most charismatic of champions, but indisputably a British one—just look at his passport. Muzza's victory in 2013 was thus greeted with what you might call a national orgasm: record TV ratings, spontaneous street parties, ecstatic headlines and noisy parades. He got a standing ovation from the prime minister, and a personal note from the Queen. He got a flower named after him by the Royal Horticultural Society, and he saw the Royal Mail issue commemorative stamps. One excited fan even had an image of Murray kissing the trophy tattooed all over his chest.

But here's the thing, folks: Murray's from Scotland. I don't mean to be a downer and all, but the fact is, England still sucks. Take a look at its best players from the past four decades, and I think you'll agree that national celebrations may not really be that appropriate. Indeed, given the Lawn Tennis Association's first-class training facilities and budget of £60 million, some sort of national suicide pact might be called for instead.

Aside from Tim Henman (who chalked up eleven career titles) and Greg Rusedski (who was born and raised in Canada), England has had just three players crack the world's top fifty in the past forty years. The best players outside of that elite group were Jeremy Bates (a doubles specialist), Andrew Castle (a mixed-doubles specialist) and Jamie Delgado (a nice person). None of these men were household names. Unless the house happened to belong to their mum.

Since Henman retired in 2007, only one English player has really made headlines: a twenty-three-year-old named Robert Dee, from Bexley in Kent. A man who managed to play on the professional tennis circuit for over three years ... without winning a single match. When Dee finally snapped his losing streak in 2008 by beating an unranked seventeen-year-old in Spain, the *Daily Telegraph* put the news on its front page: 'World's worst tennis pro wins at last,' it proudly proclaimed. 'After 54 defeats in a row, Dee has won his first match.'

An enraged Dee promptly sued the paper, arguing that to call him the 'world's worst tennis pro' was an entirely unjustified smear.

Somewhat embarrassingly, the judge disagreed.

Sad-faced Swedes

Each Grand Slam has its share of special fans—those extra-enthusiastic spectators for whom tennis is so much more than a sport. Every Wimbledon, for example, sees a selection of England's middle classes gather on Henman Hill to cheer their compatriots; and every US Open sees some truckies go to a women's match and drunkenly yell, 'Show us ya tits'. And the French crowd always provides great support for French players. Unless it doesn't happen to be in the mood. In which case it boos them.

Individual players, too, have their own special fan clubs that seem to follow them wherever they go. Watch a Lleyton Hewitt match and you'll soon hear the Fanatics. And any match between James Blake and Sam Querrey can get a little noisy, what with the J-Block and the Samurai in the stands.

But it's the Australian Open that seems to attract the most colourful fans—and the Swedish ones are the best of the bunch. While multicultural Melbourne has a blue-and-white army of Greek fans, and once hosted a riot between some Croats and Serbs, it's the smiling Swedes who've been face-painting the longest, and how can you beat that blue-and-yellow ensemble with the big Viking horns?

And historically, they've had plenty to smile about. From the mid-seventies until the early nineties, Sweden was the little nation that could. With stars like Mats Wilander, Stefan Edberg and Björn Borg leading the way, and dozens of more-than-able types like Mikael Pernfors right behind them, Swedish men won twenty-four out of a possible seventy-six Grand Slams during a nineteen-year period, not to mention four Davis Cups. In 1988, this country of nine million people had thirteen men in the world's top 100.

'I loved to watch all the Swedish players,' says Robin Söderling, the last Swedish man to make the top ten. 'I was very patriotic when I was a kid, and it was great, because every tournament there was at least one Swedish player doing good, and there was one Swedish player you could follow. That's mostly why I started to play tennis.'

Nowadays, though, Swedes have a lot less to smile about: the little nation that could has become the little nation that can't. Swedish players have managed just one Grand Slam victory since 1992 (Thomas Johansson's surprise 2002 win at the Australian Open), and only three other Swedes have managed to get to a final.

But the fans keep on cheering. Maybe they're just glad that they're not English.

Sad-faced officials

Faced, as they were, with a constant struggle for resources, it's said that the Inuit people of Eastern Siberia used to take a rather novel approach to aged care. When elderly 'Eskimos' just got too elderly, and were no longer able to help forage for food, they would set be adrift on a floating iceberg, and left to freeze to death all on their own.

All a bit grim, really. But an even more diabolical fate awaits the world's old people today. Quite a few of them end up as linespeople.

Let's just think for a moment about what the job entails: studying a rule book for days and days so they can stand in the hot sun for hours on end. Staring at a thin white line. The game itself linespeople are duty-bound to ignore, however entertaining it might happen to be.

And when I say standing, I mean bending over. So that their head is about the same height as it might otherwise be if anyone was ever nice enough to give them a chair.

As a reward for this, linespeople are given very little money—or, very often, none at all. But they do at least get plenty of criticism. All in all, it's the classic thankless task: no credit comes their way when they get a call right, but they'll see plenty of TV cameras whenever they're wrong.

The linesperson's harshest critics, of course, are the players themselves. 'I know I can see the ball better than the officials,' said John McEnroe, a famously calm and reasonable man. 'I can "feel" when a ball is out or not. What's so frustrating is to know you're right and not be able to do anything about it.' (Apart from glare, spit, scream and swear.)

David Nalbandian has also been known to share his thoughts with linespeople when the mood takes him, a habit that once got him disqualified from Queens. 'I never intended to hit him [the line judge], it was an unfortunate reaction in which I wanted to let off steam after losing a point,' Nalbandian plaintively insisted at a press conference, after he kicked an advertising board at an elderly linesman . . . and tore a long, bloody gash in the man's leg.

But for all the ordeals faced by the older generation, we should be aware that the ball kids are also doing it tough. Where once upon a time we sent children down coal mines, society's most vulnerable members are now made to scamper in the hot, cruel sun in search of little green balls.

Though often enough, the balls come straight to them. At around about 200 km per hour. Modern tennis essentially involves a lot of small, hard missiles which ball kids can quite literally cop on the chin. Type 'ball kid injuries' into YouTube and you'll see a series of gruesome atrocities that wouldn't be out of place on the Gaza Strip.

Mind you, their low social status must hurt even more. Ball kids don't just retrieve tennis balls. They also clean up stray rubbish. And hand players drinks. And pick up the sweaty towels that players thoughtlessly drop to the floor. If a player wants something done, it's the ball kid that does it. 'Last year, in a Victoria Azarenka game, a pigeon kept hitting the roof,' says a ball kid called Aiofe, who spent his years as a slave at the French Open. 'We kept having to go round and collect the feathers [because] she was getting annoyed.'

The French Open is also notable for requiring its ball kids to work eleven-hour days, and stare at their feet during every point, rather than, say, take in the game. What if a minute should pass in which they actually enjoyed themselves? *Sacre bleu* and *quelle horreur*!

But at least ball kids get to chat with their heroes. Or not. 'The players are so focused, so they don't really [speak to us or thank us],' says an Australian Open ball kid called Ella. 'I think it's the rules.'

Crazy parents

In 1998, Martina Hingis was the undisputed queen of women's tennis—but many observers were more excited by her doubles partner. Six-foot super-server Mirjana Lučić won the Australian Open doubles that year playing alongside Hingis, and reached the Wimbledon singles semifinals eighteen months later. She was just fifteen years old.

And that was as good as her career ever got.

So what happened? That question should rather be '*who* happened?', and its answer, sad to say, is, 'her dad'. Marinko Lučić's mental and physical abuse of his daughter 'left her little more than a listless puppet on the tennis court', according to the *New York Times*'s Robin Finn. 'Beatings ... there have been more of them than anyone can imagine,' she told a Zagreb newspaper,

Slobodna Dalmacijaj, not long after she fled to the United States. 'Sometimes it was because of the lost game, in other cases for the lost set or badly played trainings. I don't want to even say what happened after the matches I lost.'

In a 2003 poll conducted by a British newspaper, Marinko was voted the worst tennis parent of all time—and it has to be said that this is quite an achievement, given the stiff competition. Tennis, you see, is simply full of crazy parents: of mums and dads driven by money, ego or some kind of inherent control-freakery into systematically exploiting their offspring, and turning their childhood into some kind of boot camp. 'My overall impression down the years is that more parents have a negative effect on a young person's tennis career than have a positive influence,' says Florida supercoach Nick Bollettieri. 'Too many of them don't know what's right for their children.'

It would probably be reasonable to put Jim Pierce into this category. His daughter Mary was just eighteen when she was forced to take out a restraining order against him. And hire a bodyguard. And hide out in hotels. Some reports even suggested that Jim, a convicted felon who was fond of screaming at his daughter until she broke down in tears, threatened her life. Whether or not that is true, there's no doubt that he effectively ruined it.

But, in Jim's defence, he at least tried to be supportive during his daughter's matches, often yelling out words of encouragement such as 'Kill the bitch!' It was a habit that once got him into trouble with some fans at the French Open—but he had no problems dealing with *them*. 'One guy grabbed me and jerked me around, so I drilled him,' he proudly told the *South Florida Sun Sentinel*. 'Two of them went down [during the brawl that then erupted] and I was still standing.'

Bernard Tomic's father has also been known to express himself physically. Scarred by his experiences during the Croatian War of Independence—and, psychologically speaking, clearly a victim—John Tomic famously headbutted his young son's hitting partner, breaking his nose and damaging his vertebrae. And he's also been accused of punching Bernard himself—not to mention shooting him with a BB gun. 'John has multiple fits of anger during training,' says the hitting partner. 'Every day you never know how he is going to react to something or how he is going to behave, maybe nice, maybe not. Always it's stress, every day stress.'

John Tomic was sentenced to eight months in prison after the headbutting incident, but managed to avoid going there for even a day. The same, alas, can't be said for Steffi Graf's father, who spent a year behind bars after trying to evade tax on more than $4 million of her earnings. It wasn't the first black mark against the man nicknamed Papa Merciless, a man his daughter prefers not to discuss.

Stefano Capriati also had a hands-on approach when it came to his daughter's finances. 'Where I come from we have a proverb,' he said when she was thirteen. '"When the apple is ripe, eat it." Jennifer is ripe.' So he started ringing sponsors and made her turn pro. By the time Capriati was fifteen, she had over $10 million worth of endorsement deals ... and a depressive condition that will last the rest of her life. As a journalist once famously put it, Stefano treated his daughter as nothing more than 'a ponytailed ATM'.

To this day, we'll never know whether the salmon was ripe, but we do know that Damir Dokić refused to eat it. Once thrown out of the US Open for quarrelling about the price of a plate of fish—and then out of the Australian Open for accusing organisers of fixing the draw—Jelena Dokić's father is no more popular at Wimbledon, where he was detained by police after smashing someone's mobile phone. He's also been ejected from tournaments for calling officials 'Nazis' ... and for grabbing hold of a TV camera ... and for calling someone a cow. Other highlights of Damir's career include a fifteen-month jail term for threatening to assassinate an ambassador and keeping a collection of rifles and hand grenades in his home. In between all this, he also found time to hit his daughter. But that was 'for her sake', so that's okay.

'I've been through a lot worse than anybody on the tour. I can say that with confidence,' Jelena once told a journalist. 'There was a period where there was nothing that could make me happy. I wanted somebody else's life.'

She may not have chosen Michael Chang's, however. While the Chinese American star suffered no physical abuse, public humiliation can be painful as well. 'The ultimate tennis mother', Betty Chang was once voted the least-liked person on the ATP Tour, and her control-freakery was said to extend into every area, including the one downstairs. The story goes that Michael once received a visit from his mother after a Davis Cup work-out . . . while he was in the change room with friends. She suggested that he shower and change his clothes, having touched his underwear and reported that it was 'wet'.

Alexandra Stevenson's mum also liked to visit the locker room, but *moral* hygiene was her primary concern. She claimed that she needed to chaperone her daughter to protect her from all the lesbian players (though even some of the straight ones were 'pushy bitches').

If only someone had thought to protect the world from Christophe Fauviau. Although his children never became professional tennis players, this former French army helicopter pilot deserves a mention here for being, well, an absolute psycho. Fauviau was sent to prison for drugging his children's opponents twenty-seven times during tournaments in the early 2000s, using an anti-anxiety drug which causes drowsiness. He didn't stop when many of them collapsed during matches, or became horribly ill.

But he *did* stop after one of them drove home, complaining of drowsiness. And died in a crash on the way.

Players-turned-coaches

Endless travel and endless training. A strict diet and daily reps at the gym. From the moment they pick up a racquet as little kids with big dreams, to the day they retire (having achieved maybe two of them), tennis pros don't really *play* the sport so much as they *live* it obsessively. It really is an all-consuming career. A lifestyle that leaves little time for school (let alone university) and takes you far away from family and friends.

It's very easy to understand why so many retired tennis players eventually decide to take up coaching. Why settle down and enjoy your family when you can keep living in a hundred different hotels?

'We have what most conventional coaches don't,' says Michael Chang, who now coaches Kei Nishikori. 'We know what it's like to be on top. We've been there. We know how it works and how to react in a given situation.'

When Chang says 'we', he's not talking about himself and his mother (I believe that they are now living apart). He's talking about the glut of former Grand Slam champions who are now sitting in players' boxes all over the globe. Included among them are Stefan Edberg, who advises Roger Federer, and the two-time French Open winner Sergi Bruguera, who coaches Richard Gasquet. Goran Ivanisevic has worked with Marin Ĉilić since 2010, and Boris Becker has been coaching Novak Djokovic since the start of 2014.

'I think it's good for tennis,' says Scotland's Andy Murray, who started the trend by hiring Ivan Lendl in early 2012 to supply some 'fresh insight'. 'It's good for the players. I think it gives the sport a boost. I mean, when those guys played they played in great eras. They were all great players.'

And, of course, they look great in your box. 'I've known tennis for a few years now, and I know that when someone is doing something that works, everyone is copying,' says Serena Williams's coach, Patrick Mouratoglou. 'So two years ago everybody wanted to have this special [gluten-free] diet that Novak had, because he was winning with that diet. Now the fashion is everybody wants to have an ex–number one with him, because Andy Murray did so well with Lendl. Of course I have a lot of respect for all these champions, definitely. They have great experience to share. Players just have to be careful because being a coach is a real job.'

But *are* they getting the job done? Well, Lendl definitely did well with Murray—helping the underachieving twenty-four-year-old to his first two Slams—but it's hard to say that all of the players-turned-coaches have added all that much as yet.

'For me, it can be fantastic to have a coach that was a great player, but it's even better to look into those who were able to do great things with limited skills,' says commentator Jim Courier. 'Players like Brad Gilbert, José Higueras ... who didn't have a tremendous talent at first but who maximized their potential. In my opinion, they have the best profile to lead a player to the top.'

Players-turned-commentators

'Smith hits a cross-court forehand! Jones return it back down the line! Backhand! Backhand! Forehand! Backhand! And Smith's forehand return goes into the net. First point to Brown. Fifteen–Love.'

If you've ever heard tennis commentary on the radio, I'm pretty sure that you turned it straight off.

That leaves us with *TV* commentary. For that, you generally need to press 'mute'. Most TV viewers know a serve when they see it, and will tend to notice whether or not the other player has managed to hit a return, so the role of a TV commentator is not to describe every single thing that happens in a match, but to make sense of it all with some 'special comments'. While some former players do this well (Jim Courier and Billie Jean King, among them), there are plenty of others whose comments aren't really that special at all.

Sin number one is stating the obvious. If I had a dollar for every time a 'tactical expert' suggested that a player should 'change it up' and 'attack the net', I'd have enough money to buy a 51 per cent share of Facebook and close it down for the good of mankind.

Equally, when a player makes a crucial error, we really don't need to be told that he or she 'wouldn't have wanted to do that'. And while it's always good to know that 'we haven't had any more rain since it stopped raining' (thank you, Harry Carpenter), Ann Jones probably didn't need to tell us that 'when Chrissie [Evert] is playing well, I always feel that she is playing well'.

Sin two is pointless predictions. If a player wins the first two sets, I think we're all aware that they're on track for the match. And it was also hard to disagree with Martina Navratilova at Wimbledon when she said, 'I had a feeling today that Venus Williams would either win or lose.'

Sin three is excessive cross-promotion: commentators who take every single opportunity to tell viewers about some of their TV network's upcoming shows. Though on the whole, it's better than *self*-promotion, when commentators take every opportunity to wax lyrical about their own glory days.

But perhaps I am being unfair here. It's wrong to tar all commentators with this one manky brush. Some of them have provided some genuinely special comments over the years. Take Virginia Wade, for example, who's a master of the arresting metaphor. 'She's got several layers of steel out there like a cat with nine lives,' Wade once told TV viewers, while another player needed 'to take her nerves by the horns'.

Perhaps Wade herself was getting a bit nervous? If only she could be more like Ivan Lendl and Martina Navratilova. According to the BBC commentator Dan Maskell, Lendl could be 'as calm as the proverbial iceberg'. And 'when Martina is tense, it helps her relax'.

Dan Maskell was also known to admire Slobodan Živojinović, a big-serving Serbian who nearly always managed to 'pull the big bullet out of the top drawer'. Which is a pretty impressive talent, given how skinny he must have been ('And here's Živojinović, six foot six inches tall and fourteen pounds, ten ounces.')

But Maskell was certainly not the only 'special comments' man who specialised in making no sense. 'Strawberries, cream and champers flow like hot cakes' at Wimbledon, according to one BBC reporter, and so do non sequiturs, malapropisms and gaffes. Take the following:

- 'This is the third week the fish seem to be getting away from British tennis players.' *Gerald Williams*
- 'Lloyd did what he achieved with that shot.' *Jack Bannister*
- 'Billie Jean King [has a] look on her face that says she can't believe it … because she never believes it, and yet, somehow, I think she does.' *Max Robertson*
- 'Strangely enough, Kathy Jordan is getting to the net first, which she always does.' *Fred Perry*
- 'McEnroe has got to sit down and work out where he stands.' *Fred Perry*
- 'If she gets the jitters now, then she isn't the great champion that she is.' *Max Robertson*
- 'Chip Hooper is such a big man that it is sometimes difficult to see where he is on the court.' *Mark Cox*
- 'Those two volleys really could be the story of this match summed up at the end of it.' *Barry Davies*
- 'He's got his hands on his knees and holds his head in despair.' *Peter Jones*
- 'These ball boys are marvellous. You don't even notice them. There's a left-handed one over there. I noticed him earlier.' *Max Robertson*
- 'It's quite clear that Virginia Wade is thriving on the pressure now that the pressure on her to do well is off.' *Harry Carpenter*

The commentator Ann Jones once praised a player for 'keeping her head beautifully on her shoulders.' If only she could say the same thing about some of her colleagues.

4

THE GRAND CHAMPIONS – MEN

'It's impossible to compare different players from different eras' is a phrase you'll often hear from slightly boring people, and it's a phrase that may well be true.

But it is also impossible to publish a book that doesn't actually contain any words. Here, then, are some players that many people regard as some of history's best. Other books may list other greats, but it appears that you bought this book instead. Thanks for that, by the way. Now, please read on.

Bill Tilden

'When I missed, I was surprised,' William Tatem Tilden II once said of his tennis game, and he was far from the only one. A relatively late starter at the sport, and a man who wasn't even selected to play for his Ivy League college, this wealthy descendant of William the Conqueror hit his straps after WWI. And hit ace, after ace, after ace.

With a booming serve that once clocked 260 km per hour, 'Big Bill' won 138 of the 192 tournaments he entered during the twenties and thirties, the vast majority with contemptuous ease. During 1924, he won every single match he played. The following year, he won fifty-seven in a row.

But it was the *way* he won that really got people talking. A man who loved a rally for its own sake, and was always thinking at least three shots ahead, Tilden didn't like to outmuscle his opponents so much as out*smart* them. 'When you played Tilden, you had to think,' said Fred Perry, the last Englishman to ever win Wimbledon. 'I learned a great deal from him. See, when you played Bill, you never got anything you wanted. If you wanted it low, he gave it to you high. If you wanted it wide, he gave it to you close. If you wanted it fast he gave it to you slow. If you wanted to talk, he shut up. If you wanted to play silently, he talked. You were always thinking, and you had to think against Tilden.'

And if you were a spectator, you just had to applaud. A would-be poet and thespian (who eventually lost most of his money backing bad Broadway plays), Tilden liked to bow to the crowd whenever he hit a winner, and he wore monogrammed white jackets long before the Fed. 'The player owes the gallery as much as an actor owes the audience,' was the view of this flamboyant fashionista, who would often prolong a rally for the sake of the show.

'He is an artist,' Franklin Adams wrote in 1921. 'He is more of an artist than nine-tenths of the artists I know. It is the beauty of the game that Tilden loves. It is the chase always, rather than the quarry.'

'To his opponents, it was a contest,' is how Paul Gallico put it, rather less kindly. 'With Tilden, it was an expression of his own tremendous and overwhelming ego, coupled with feminine vanity.'

The artist ditched his amateur status at the age of thirty-seven, a few weeks after becoming the oldest man to ever win Wimbledon. (He would have won many more Wimbledons had he not found the tournament so boring, incidentally, and so for five years had not made the trip.) But while Tilden was one of the first players to earn serious money from the fledgling professional tour, he was a pretty serious spender as well. Bad investments and a great lifestyle saw him slowly slip into poverty—and in the 1940s he faced notoriety as well. A lifelong 'bachelor', Tilden's reputation was destroyed when he was found guilty of a morals charge in connection with a teenage boy. He served seven months of a year-long jail term, only to be jailed again for picking up a sixteen-year-old boy.

Some people say that there's no such thing as bad publicity—but, believe me, they are wrong. Shunned by the tennis establishment—he was even banned from giving lessons at local clubs—Big Bill died of a heart attack three years after his release from prison, with exactly eighty-eight bucks in the bank. The ten-time Grand Slam winner's name has been more or less wiped from tennis history, and you won't see it on too many honour boards today.

The audience had packed up and gone home.

Nicknames: 'Big Bill', 'Gentleman Bill'

Nationality: American

Date of birth: 10 February 1893

Strengths: Speed, court smarts

Weakness: Fond of sex with minors

Grand Slams: French Open (1927, 1930)
    Wimbledon (1920–21, 1930)
    US Open (1920–25, 1929)

In his own words: 'Never change a winning game; always change a losing one.'

In somebody else's: 'He carved up his opponents as a royal chef would carve meat to the king's taste. He was the most striking and commanding figure the game of tennis had ever put on court.' *John Keiran*

Donald Budge

For most of us suburban tennis players, backhands are far and away the game's hardest shot. Our basic aim is to not embarrass ourselves. It's just a bonus if it goes over the net.

And things weren't actually all that different for the world's best tennis players, way back in the game's early days. With the small-headed wooden racquets that they had to use, together with not-very-bouncy balls, the backhand was mostly a defensive shot—a dainty prod or a cautious poke; certainly not a full-blooded swing.

But in the 1930s, somebody changed all that (and if you ask me, he should have changed his name, too). Donald Budge's backhand was his number one asset—a *weapon*, rather than something to hide. 'Probably the single most ravaging stroke the game has seen', it was fast, flat, hit with an unusually heavy racquet, and almost entirely devoid of spin. One player swore that he could read the ball-maker's logo whenever Budge hit his signature shot. Other players probably could, too, only Budge kept hitting it past them so bloody fast.

Where did he learn how to do it? The answer is probably the baseball field: his 'money stroke ... grew directly out of his almost-perfect, left-handed batting swings', according to a journalist of the day.

Basketball was another childhood passion of the super-talented sportsman, along with soccer and American football. Indeed, Budge barely played any tennis at all until the age of fourteen, when his brother suggested that he enter the California State Boys Championship—which, with barely a week's practice, he won.

Seven years later, he was the world's best player. A tall, skinny redhead, with big ears and a protruding nose, 'Donnie' won Wimbledon and the US Open in 1937, and led his country to a famous Davis Cup win. Then in 1938, he achieved the world's first Grand Slam, losing just five sets over all four tournaments.

No-one will ever know what he might have gone on to accomplish, because the following year, at the very height of his powers, there occurred a little-known event we call World War II. Travel to England, France and Australia was now impossible, and those countries in any case had no Grand Slams to play. The United States entered the war in 1942, and Budge duly entered the army, and injured his shoulder. He played the occasional match after the war was all over, but could never quite recover his unbeatable form.

But Budge still has an unbeatable reputation. Far more than just a big backhand, he had a blistering serve and plenty of court speed, a pretty good forehand and an excellent smash. 'Playing tennis against him was like playing against a concrete wall,' said one opponent, Sidney Wood. 'There was nothing to attack.'

He was 'almost unplayable at times', as Great Britain's 'Bunny' Austin remembers it. 'It was an honour just to be on the same court.'

Nickname: 'Donnie'

Nationality: American

Date of birth: 13 June 1915

Strengths: Backhand

Weakness: Parents named him Donald

Grand Slams: Australian Open (1938)
French Open (1938)
Wimbledon (1937–38)
US Open (1937–38)

In his own words: 'I patterned my game after Vines and Perry; then I turned it up a notch.'

In somebody else's: 'Budge was the best of all. He owned the most perfect set of mechanics and he was the most consistent.' *Jack Kramer*

Ricardo 'Pancho' Gonzales

'If Earth was on the line in a tennis match,' wrote a journalist in *Sports Illustrated*, 'the man you want serving to save humankind would be Ricardo Alonso Gonzalez.'

A player who spent the vast majority of his career on the professional circuit, and so only managed to clock up a couple of Slams, 'Pancho' Gonzalez is thought to have had tennis's best-ever serve (or at least its second best, behind Pete Sampras).

'Marvellously pure and effortless', it was 'the most beautiful service motion of them all'—able to go fast, flat and wide; or loop, swerve or slice; or do all those things seemingly at once. With groundstrokes that were 'sufficient but not spectacular', Gonzales could sometimes struggle to break his opponent's serve, but he very rarely lost his own.

Pancho's reflexes and speed were also a strength: his nickname could have easily been 'Panther'. 'Gonzales is the greatest natural athlete tennis has ever known,' said long-time rival Tony Trabert, who also considered him to be the sport's greatest knob. 'The way he can move that six-foot-three-inch frame of his around the court is almost unbelievable. He's just like a big cat.'

But 'rival' may be generous word for Trabert: Pancho beat him seventy-four times in the 101 pro games they played. He also carved out an embarrassingly good record against the likes of Lew Hoad, Ken Rosewall and Frank Sedgman during the years that those amateur stars played pro. Pancho simply dominated the pro circuit for over two decades. He even beat Rod Laver at the ripe old age of forty-two.

'He was a marvellous player, a great competitor,' said Laver's fellow Grand Slam champion Don Budge. 'He was the best player who never won Wimbledon.'

He was probably also the most unlikeable player to have never won Wimbledon—and, when you think about it, that's quite an achievement. Loathed by opponents (and thus loved by promoters), Pancho was the quintessential bad guy—a sort of pantomime villain with a big nasty scar and big bulging muscles, a foul temper and a menacing scowl.

'We felt that he hated us and that he hated himself,' said Laver of 'the lone wolf', who more or less spent his life in a series of feuds. 'He was willing to do anything to win a match, even to intimidate the referees, players and spectators. He was a real wild guy, with an incredible petulant streak. After a defeat,

I remember seeing him seriously damaging iron cabinets or breaking everything in the dressing rooms. But he played much better when he was edgy than when he was calm.'

'Gonzales is very even-tempered,' is how Pancho Segura put it. 'He is always mad.'

A Californian born to poor Mexican immigrants, and by all reports 'difficult' at school, Gonzales taught himself to play tennis as a twelve-year-old, after his mum bought him a fifty-cent racquet. A promising career was put on hold when he was arrested for burglary at fifteen and put in detention for over a year. And after that, he spent two years in the Navy, only to be dishonourably discharged.

Pancho was nineteen and unemployable—but with that fifty-cent racquet, he was unplayable, too. With no other option open to him, unless you count poverty or jail, Gonzales started entering tennis tournaments, and within two years he'd won two US Opens. But what he *hadn't* won was nearly enough money—so the twenty-one-year-old turned his back on tennis superstardom, and decided to turn pro instead.

Had he stayed amateur, there's no telling how many Slams he'd have won. Or how many players he would have terrified in the process.

Nicknames: 'Pancho', 'That bastard', 'That prick', 'That arsehole'

Nationality: American

Date of birth: 9 May 1928

Strengths: Cannonball serve, natural athleticism

Weakness: Ever so slightly unhinged

Grand Slams: US Open (1948–49)

In his own words: 'The great champions were always vicious competitors.'

In somebody else's: 'At five-all in the fifth, there's no man in the history of tennis I'd bet against him.' *Jack Kramer*

Rod Laver

'Rocket' Rod Laver's nickname was actually ironic. The young Queenslander got it because he was so slow.

And the way he looked didn't exactly scream 'strength' either. The short, skinny son of a cattle farmer, Laver nearly died from hepatitis as a small child, and spent much of his career looking like he still could. He was pale and frail, with bow legs and a sallow face. He had freckles, a bent nose and red hair. If he was a racehorse, you wouldn't have bet on him; you would have called a vet and had him put down.

So what made Laver so good? So, well, All-Time-Great. Well, for a start, he was muscly where it counted. Rocket had the left arm of a heavyweight boxer—a musclebound limb 'so much larger than his right that it appeared deformed'—and he had a thick left wrist that was 'iron clad'. 'The strength of that wrist and forearm gave him blazing power without loss of control,' wrote the journalist Rex Bellamy, 'even when he was on the run and at full stretch. The combination of speed and strength, especially wrist strength, enabled him to hit ferocious winners when way out of court.'

But Laver certainly wasn't all about power. He was also about timing and, above all, spin. 'The Rockhampton Rocket' should really be called 'The Wristy Groundstroke': he was the first player to really *flick* the ball, the first to consistently use topspin to give his shots that extra little bit of loop. Every player uses topspin nowadays but before Rod, almost nobody did. Before Rod, it was a different game. He wasn't just very good at tennis. He helped to reinvent it.

Self-taught on a homemade court that his farmer dad made out of ant beds, Laver had a bag of tricks that went beyond topspin. From attacking lobs and defensive drop shots, to ridiculous angles that no-one saw coming, he was a man who could hit every shot in the book, plus a few more that need to go in the sequel. 'Laver was technically faultless,' said the commentator Dan Maskell, 'from his richly varied serve to his feather-light touch on drop volleys plus a backhand drive carrying destructive topspin when needed or controlling slice when the occasion demanded it.'

But unfortunately Laver did have one fault. He chose to play much of his career on the pro tour. When he turned pro at the age of twenty-three, he had already won six Grand Slam titles—four of them in the one calendar year. Who knows what records might have been broken next, had he not then spent his prime playing meaningless exhibition matches in front of small crowds in the American suburbs?

All we do know is that the Open Era began in 1968, and Rocket Rod was finally allowed to rejoin the tour. Aged thirty, he became Wimbledon's first Open Era champion that year, and was the runner-up in the very first French Open. And the year after that, he won all four Grand Slams—becoming the first and (still) the only person to ever complete the Grand Slam twice.

And that, my friends, is quite a career—however you want to spin it.

Nickname: 'The Rockhampton Rocket'

Nationality: Australian

Date of birth: 9 August 1938

Strength: Topspin forehand

Weaknesses: None (note: author is also Australian)

Grand Slams: Australian Open (1960, 1962, 1969)
French Open (1962, 1969)
Wimbledon (1961–62, 1968–69)
US Open (1962, 1969)

In his own words: 'The time your game is most vulnerable is when you're ahead; never let up.'

In somebody else's: 'You take all the criteria—longevity, playing on grass and clay, amateur, professional, his behaviour, his appearance—in all criteria, Laver's the best player of all time.' *Ted Schroeder*

Björn Borg

There's something extra alluring about great talents who tragically depart at their peak: JFK, Janis Joplin, Jim Morrison, Marilyn Monroe. We never see them fade and we never see them grow fat. They never bald, they never slow, they never sag. In our minds, they're all still superstars: forever groovy and shiny and young.

Tennis's (albeit still alive) example of this interesting phenomenon is a Swedish man called Björn Borg. An all-conquering megastar with an excellent haircut who walked away from the game at age twenty-six. Who walked away after winning five consecutive Wimbledons and six French Opens, and reaching the final of the US Open four times.

'I didn't enjoy it,' the Swede says simply, about the sport he started playing professionally at the age of fourteen. 'My focus was not there.' And focus was what this ultra-fit baseliner was all about (well, okay: focus and excellent haircuts). Never one to reveal what was going on in his mind (if, indeed, anything was), Borg's ice-cold composure earned him the nickname 'the Ice Borg'.

'I try to make my challenger believe he can't out-steady me,' the Iceman once said of his ever-chilly demeanour on court. 'I never applaud or acknowledge an opponent's good shot, I just go about the business of the next point. This, in a sense, is saying, "I don't care how spectacular one shot is, you'll have to hit two thousand to beat me."'

And, just like the one that hit the *Titanic*, the iceberg from Sweden caused some pretty damn big names to sink. A little bit blah to watch, Borg's game was based on power and consistency: on big, heavy topspin groundstrokes hit again and again like a carpenter hammering a nail. But while players like Laver had used topspin before, no-one had ever thought to use it this much. Borg hardly ever lobbed and rarely ever sliced and when he approached the net, it was just to shake hands. 'We're playing tennis,' as Ilie Năstase once put it, 'and he's playing something else.'

But whatever he was doing, the crowds liked it. With his stylish clothes and long, blonde locks, his hot model girlfriends and designer stubble, Borg was well and truly the first tennis rock star, and every magazine editor's (slightly wet) dream. 'He was bigger than the game,' said Arthur Ashe. 'He was like Elvis or Liz Taylor or somebody.'

'All those girls, all those teenagers,' recalls the man himself, who often had to hide in his hotel room while hormonal adolescents had hysterics outside: 'It was kind of a rock thing, a music thing. It was a new thing for tennis. It was a new thing for me.'

And, presumably, it was quite an exhausting thing. Borg 'didn't feel young when he quit', is how the commentator Mary Carillo put it.

He was happy to feel up the young, though. One of Borg's first acts on retiring was to help judge a wet T-shirt competition … and then father a child with a seventeen-year-old contestant. The affair ended the first of his three marriages, and provided one of the highlights in a post-tennis career that has also featured bankruptcy and a rumoured drug overdose.

The key to Borg's tennis, according to his coach, was 'not the way he came to master his ground strokes, but the change he underwent, with terrible determination, to tame his passionate spirit.'

It would seem that, under all that ice, there was fire.

Pete Sampras

In 1999, the world's number one player, Pete Sampras, won a world-record sixth Wimbledon crown. He won the final in three straight sets, and even took out match point with a second serve ace.

'What was going through your mind before that serve?' breathless reporters asked the champ at the subsequent press conference.

'There was absolutely nothing going through my mind,' he steadily replied.

There have been more charismatic tennis champions than 'Pistol' Pete Sampras. To be honest, there have been more charismatic tables. Once described by Agassi as being 'more robotic than a parrot', Sampras never smashed a racquet or swore at an umpire or belittled an opponent or made an excuse. He just went about the business of training and winning, and occasionally took some time out to work on his golf. His was a perfect game played with perfect politeness. And, like all perfection, it was deeply dull.

But if Pete had all the personality of a suburban accountant, it's important to add that he had the game of an angel. A beautiful volleyer, with stylish, fluent groundstrokes, he had perhaps the best first serve in the history of tennis, and his second serve was very nearly as good. Rumour has it that Sampras would place coins on the court and practise hitting them to improve his accuracy. And whether or not that's true, he could hit aces at will.

'When Pete is playing his best, he's practically impossible to pass,' Michael Chang once said of his compatriot, who came across a tennis racquet in his basement as a toddler and learned the game by hitting balls against the wall. 'What can you do?

Maybe go over the net and break his strings? Pete has one weakness though, he can't cook.'

Jealousy may be another weakness, however: before Federer came along, Sampras was widely regarded as the best player of the modern tennis era, if not the best player of all time. And fair enough too. He won fourteen Grand Slam titles, after all, and was world number one for six consecutive years. He was, quite simply, a winning machine—albeit one that tended to break down when the surface was clay. The French Open is the one gap on Pete's glittering CV. But hey, it's a gap on mine too.

But again we get back to the machine analogy. No piece on Sampras can avoid it for too long. In his autobiography, he criticised the way that 'some people took it upon themselves to interpret my extraordinary self-control as evidence of a lack of emotion. This struck me as pretty arrogant. I had emotions, alright, trust me on that; I just knew how to master them.'

He certainly chose an emotional way to retire. After his Wimbledon winning streak was ended by a Swiss up-and-comer named Federer, most people saw Sampras as finished. And they

Nickname: 'Pistol Pete'

Nationality: American

Date of birth: 12 August 1971

Strengths: Serve, volleys

Weakness: Duller than dishwater

Grand Slams: Australian Open (1994, 1997)
Wimbledon (1993–95, 1997–2000)
US Open (1993, 1993, 1995–96, 2002)

In his own words: 'I never wanted to be the great guy or the colourful guy or the interesting guy. I wanted to be the guy who won titles.'

In somebody else's: 'His temperament in big matches is phenomenal.' *Rod Laver*

didn't change their mind over the following twelve months, when he won absolutely nothing at all.

But—seeded seventeenth and long past his prime—Sampras then managed to shock everyone by winning the 2002 US Open in a final against Andre Agassi. The man with whom he had had a career-long rivalry. And the man he had defeated to win his very first Slam.

It was a wonderfully symbolic time to call it quits, so this consummate showman did just that.

Twelve months later.

Roger Federer

Seventeen grand slam titles. Over $80 million in prize money. Three hundred weeks as world number one. Swiss star Roger Federer was once asked how he kept managing to perform at such a consistently high level. 'You know, there's no secret about it,' he calmly replied. 'I'm definitely a very talented player.'

Not, perhaps, the most modest of answers, but it's pretty hard to disagree. In an era of power tennis—of whackers and thwackers and thunkers and clunkers—Federer stands alone as a pure tennis stylist; as a man who uses placement and variety to slice apart his opponents, rather than just hurt them with strength. The Maestro has every shot there is, and he brings them to the court every time he plays. A Federer match is a thing of beauty. A thing of topspin and backspin and no-spin; of unexpected angles and changes of pace. He can chip, charge and volley; he can grind out a rally; and he can hammer a winner from the back of the court. He simply plays great on every single surface, and he's never less than great to watch.

'He's the most gifted player that I've ever seen in my life,' says John McEnroe of the man who has reached an astonishing thirty-five Grand Slam semifinals. 'I've seen a lot of people play. I've seen the [Rod] Lavers, I played against some of the great players—the Samprases, Beckers, Connors, Borgs, you name it. This guy could be the greatest of all time.'

And as far as Laver himself is concerned, he definitely is. 'Federer certainly is my claim to be the best of all time, if there is such a thing,' said the Australian in 2007. 'He's got too many shots, too much talent in one body. It's hardly fair that one person can do all this—his backhands, his forehands, volleys, serving, his court position. The way he moves around the court, you feel like he's barely touching the ground. That's the sign of a great champion. The best way to beat him would be to hit him over the head with a racquet.'

But that doesn't seem to be a tactic that anyone's too keen to try. Fluent in four languages, and friendly in all of them, Federer is also a seven-time winner of the Stefan Edberg Sportsmanship Award—a sort of popularity contest voted for by the players. 'He is never high and mighty in the locker room or anything like that,' says Federer's whipping boy, Andy Roddick, who managed

Nicknames: 'Fed Express', 'Maestro', 'GOAT' (Greatest Of All Time)

Nationality: Swiss

Date of birth: 8 August 1981

Strengths: Pretty much everything

Weakness: Would-be fashionista

Grand Slams: Australian Open (2004, 2006–07, 2010)
French Open (2009)
Wimbledon (2003–07, 2009, 2012)
US Open (2004–08)

In his own words: 'What I think I've been able to do well over the years is play with pain, play with problems, play in all sorts of conditions.'

In somebody else's: 'In an era of specialists, you're either a clay court specialist, a grass court specialist, or a hard court specialist … or you're Roger Federer.' *Jimmy Connors*

to beat the champ just three times in twenty-four attempts. ('I'd love to hate you,' he once told Federer. 'But you're really nice.')

Rafael Nadal, on the other hand, is not one of Federer's whipping boys. So widely praised is the Swiss superstar, it feels almost wrong to point out that he may *not* in fact be the best player of all time ... or even the best player of his day. Federer has won fewer than a third of his thirty-three games against Nadal, a player who will probably end up winning even more Slams.

That's no way to end a section on the most aesthetically pleasing player of all time. But unfortunately, that's also life.

Rafael Nadal

If Roger Federer's game is a thing of beauty, then Rafael Nadal is the beast. Eighty-five kilograms of pure, bulging muscle, the Spanish baseliner hits the ball as hard as anyone in history—and manages to be one of the game's all-time great runners as well.

'He's a very special athlete with abnormal amounts of energy and explosiveness,' says Dr Angel Ruíz-Cotorro of the 'King of Clay', whose astonishing stamina has seen him grind out eight consecutive French Opens—and inevitably led to accusations of doping. 'He mixes the explosive pace of a 200-metre runner with the resistance of a marathon runner.'

And these days, it's definitely worth noting, he also likes to mix up his shots. An actually quite capable volleyer who is increasingly employing slice, touch and changes of pace, Nadal has become more than a big-hitting baseliner who simply sets up camp at the back of the court.

Just, perhaps, not *much* more ... Nadal's strength is still very much his strength, as it allows him to generate an extraordinary amount of topspin. American sports scientist John Yandell has been using special software and a high-speed video camera to measure topspin since the days of Sampras and Agassi. Those two superstars both hit the ball at around 1800 revolutions a minute, while Federer tends to average 2700. Nadal, in contrast, averages *3200* revolutions a minute—and he's been known to give 5000 a nudge. It's a skill that, in combination with his stamina, makes him far and away the greatest clay court player of all time. He's won over 93 per cent of his matches on the surface, a record that may not be broken for hundreds of years.

But the Spaniard has won on plenty of other surfaces as well—most notably on Wimbledon's grass. At the time of writing, Nadal has won fourteen Grand Slam titles, fifty-six other tournaments, four Davis Cups, and an Olympic gold medal. And he's still only twenty-eight. It's an astonishing record for someone playing in the era of Roger Federer, Andy Murray, Marat Safin and Novak Djokovic. It's an astonishing record, full stop.

As far as Andre Agassi is concerned, Nadal is already the best player of all time, regardless of how many Slams he ends up with. John McEnroe, too, recently anointed him 'the greatest player that ever lived', though this happened about three years after he said the same thing about Federer.

Nicknames: 'Rafa', 'The King of Clay', 'The Spanish Bull'

Nationality: Spanish

Date of birth: 3 June 1986

Strengths: Strength, fitness, 'lasso-whip' forehand

Weakness: Needs to adjust underpants between every point

Grand Slams: Australian Open (2009)
French Open (2005–14)
Wimbledon (2008, 2010)
US Open (2010, 2013)

In his own words: 'You just try to play tough and focus point for point. Sounds so boring, but it's the right thing to do out there.'

In somebody else's: 'It's just remarkable to me what he has done, and he has done it all during Federer's prime.' *Andre Agassi*

What most of us will be saying a few decades from now will largely depend on how Nadal's body holds up. If he stays fit and injury-free, he's on track to surpass Federer's seventeen Slams. But his may not be a game that ages particularly well. Strength fades with age, and speed goes even quicker, and Nadal's hard-running style has already half ruined his knees. Many doubt that he'll be winning Slams at thirty.

Quite frankly, he could be struggling to walk.

5

THE GRAND CHAMPIONS – WOMEN

Ginger Rogers, as many feminists like to say, did everything that the more celebrated Fred Astaire ever managed to do—except she did it backwards and wearing high heels.

Women's tennis, I point out in a similar spirit, has been underappreciated for far too long. There have been some pretty extraordinary players in its 100-year history, not least the eight I write about here.

Though, for the record, they all played in the regular way, and wore sports shoes with flat, rubber soles.

Suzanne Lenglen

There have been some great tennis nicknames over the years, from 'Boom Boom' Becker to 'Pistol Pete'. 'The Scud', the 'Superbrat' and the 'Swiss Miss' are far better names for Mark Philippoussis, John McEnroe and Martina Hingis than, well, Mark Philippoussis, John McEnroe and Martina Hingis.

But while 'Fraulein Forehand' suited Steffi Graf, and Ivan Lendl really could be 'Ivan the Terrible', the best nickname of all belongs to the Frenchwoman who fundamentally secured women's place in the sport. Suzanne 'The Goddess' Lenglen was more than the most famous female tennis player in the world for a while there. She was the most famous player of either gender. And the most famous player of any sport.

A French Open finalist at the age of fourteen—just four years after picking up her first racquet—Lenglen went on to dominate the game during the 1920s like no player before or since. She lost just one match between 1919 and 1927, and won several tournaments without losing a game. This was a woman who didn't so much defeat her opponents as *destroy* them, body and soul. They were like puppets on her racquet strings, and not very good puppets at that.

'She owned every kind of shot, plus a genius for knowing how and when to use them,' recalled her doubles partner Elizabeth Ryan (as a team, they were never beaten). 'Her game was all placement and deception and steadiness ... She never gave an opponent the same kind of shot to hit twice in a row.'

'She felt about a love set as a painter does about his masterpiece,' adds Janet Flanner. 'Each ace serve was a form of brushwork to her, and her fantastically accurate shot-placing was certainly a study in composition.'

Lenglen seemed to attract this kind of hyperbole: journalists didn't tend to *describe* her games so much as gush about them. 'Her movement, it comes across as something of a fairy,' wrote Larry Engelmann. 'She walks like a ballerina on her toes. She moves so lightly. Just grace. Pure grace. And people would point out, she was not beautiful until she started moving around the court—and then you tended to forget her lack of beauty. Have you ever seen an ugly ballerina? I don't think so, and that may be how this worked for Suzanne.'

Lenglen (who did indeed study ballet and gymnastics) attracted a lot of attention for her appearance—and you'd have to say that she sought it out, too. Whatever the weather, she would always walk onto the court with a stylish fur coat, a sexy short skirt and some long painted fingernails. She smoked, she swore, she had numerous lovers. She disputed line calls and refused to play before noon. She cried when things were going badly, and when she needed a break she drank brandy on court. She played with bare arms in an era when even men wore long sleeves, and declared that 'the fox-trot and the shimmy were excellent training for tennis'.

In short, she was a walking headline: a *Great Gatsby*–style 1920s flapper with a dollop of French diva and a talent that would not be denied. The Goddess ended her amateur career not long after playing 'the Match of the Century' against an up-and-coming prodigy called Helen Wills. Lenglen won—Lenglen *always* won—but that match may have given her a glimpse of the future, and led her to decide that it wasn't one that she liked.

In any case, she definitely liked money. In 1926, the Goddess became the first major tennis player to turn professional, accepting an offer of $50,000 from an American promoter to abandon her amateur status and play exhibitions in that country for cash.

'I have worked as hard at my career as any man or woman has worked at any career,' was her response to the resultant media outrage, 'and in my whole lifetime I have not earned $5,000—not one cent of that by my specialty, my life study—tennis. I am twenty-seven and not wealthy. Should I embark on any other career and leave the one for which I have what people call genius? Or should I smile at the prospect of actual poverty and continue to earn a fortune—for whom? Under these absurd and antiquated amateur rulings, only a wealthy person can compete, and the fact of the matter is that only wealthy people do compete. Is that fair? Does it advance the sport? Does it make tennis more popular—or does it tend to suppress and hinder an enormous amount of tennis talent lying dormant in the bodies of young men and women whose names are not in the social register?'

(If you're wondering, the answers are: 'no', 'no' and 'the second one'.)

In the end, Lenglen's professional career lasted just the one year. She retired in 1927 to set up a tennis school in Paris, write a few books and generally kick back. 'Now let me live a little,' was her final plea to the media—but she should have instead made it to fate. The Goddess died of leukaemia in her late thirties, not long after losing her sight.

Helen Wills

Helen Wills never had a tennis lesson—but you'd have to say that she handed out plenty of them over the course of her two-decade career. The daughter of a high-society surgeon, who learnt the game by playing against men at her local tennis club, Wills didn't even drop a set between 1927 and 1932, and left the game with no fewer than nineteen Grand Slams.

The key to her game was power. Wills didn't have a whole lot of subtlety; just the ability to hit the ball hard from the baseline, and then do it all over again. She would send her opponents scurrying from corner to corner until eventually she hit a winner, or—far more likely—they made a mistake. It was effective, but it wasn't pretty. While Suzanne Lenglen had treated the court like her canvas, a place for deft little touches and splashes of colour, her successor at the top treated it more like an anvil: something to batter and batter repeatedly, and then batter a little bit more.

But perhaps I do 'Little Miss Poker Face' an injustice. Because she also had another weapon: her poker face. As the

New York Times writer Allison Danzig put it, 'While power under control and the ability to hit the ball harder than any other woman on the courts were responsible for the rise of Miss Wills, the ability to mask her feelings, to maintain an inscrutable countenance in the face of the vicissitudes of match play, was the characteristic that made the deepest impression upon the tennis galleries.'

Wills was, in other words, a machine. A machine that never laughed, or smiled, or frowned, or spoke; but just won matches and walked off the court. 'I had one thought and that was to put the ball across the net,' Wills once said of her famously focused demeanour, which often caused match points to pass by unnoticed. 'I was simply myself, too deeply concentrated on the game for any extraneous thought.'

But while this whole one-point-at-a-time thing might have been a great way to win games, it was no way to win over the crowds. Helen's habit of ignoring everything around her—her opponent, her supporters, her make-up, her hair—made her increasingly unpopular with the fickle public. They called her 'Queen Helen' and 'the Imperial Helen', and even 'the Garbo of tennis'.

But like Garbo, she was just misunderstood. 'Helen was really an unconfident and awkward girl—you have no idea how awkward,' said her fellow player Hazel Hotchkiss Wightman. 'I thought of Helen as an honestly shy person who was bewildered by how difficult it was to please most people.'

'Helen was a very private person,' confirmed Kitty Godfree, 'and she didn't really make friends very much.'

And it's worth noting that inside that cold, steely tennis machine there beat the soul of an artist—a culture vulture who exhibited paintings in galleries, befriended Frida Kahlo and earned a degree in fine arts. Wills also wrote poetry and published a mystery novel. She had a personality, it just wasn't on show.

Wills's career came to an end in 1938, thanks to a small fox terrier that attacked her pet dog. In the ensuing dog fight, the index figure on her right hand was bitten—and it never quite healed. 'So that was the end of my career. I couldn't manage,' she commented blithely in a rare interview at age eighty-eight, four years before she passed away, single and childless.

At her request, no funeral service was held.

Nickname: 'Little Miss Poker Face'

Nationality: American

Date of birth: 6 October 1905

Strengths: Powerful forehand, rarely made mistakes

Weakness: Kinda forgettable

Grand Slams: French Open (1928–30, 1932)
Wimbledon (1927–30, 1932–33, 1935, 1938)
US Open (1923–25, 1927–29, 1931)

In her own words: 'When I play, I become entirely absorbed in the game.'

In other people's: 'A machine … with implacable concentration and undeniable skill.' *Helen Jacobs*

Margaret Court

Debates about the greatest female tennis player of all time generally focus on Navratilova and Graf. You might occasionally hear someone make an argument for Serena Williams, or a mythical Monica Seles-if-she-hadn't-been-stabbed. But what you won't ever hear are the stats.

The stats say that a gangly, shy girl from Western Australia won twenty-four Grand Slam singles titles. Not to mention another thirty-eight playing doubles and mixed doubles. No player was more dominant in the 1960s; perhaps no player has been more dominant, ever. The stats say that best player of all time was a serve-volleyer called Margaret Court.

Court played with a game that was very much of our time, a game based on fitness and power. 'A superbly athletic animal,' as *Sports Illustrated*'s Gwilym Brown put it, who was 'the physical equal of a great many men'. She was one of the first female players to really commit to weights training, and had a cardio regime that would kill me in a week. Nearly six feet tall—and that was no small feat in the 1960s—'the Aussie Amazon' also had arms that were a full three inches longer than you'd expected for a woman her height, a genetic advantage that gave her serves a little extra velocity, and her volleys a little extra reach. Imagine playing tennis with Mr Tickle. That was Margaret Court manning the net.

But for all the *192* titles Court won with her heavy serves, crisp volleys and reliable groundstrokes, she could have won even more if she'd had a different mindset—or, at least, that's what she maintains today. 'I was very shy [and] I had an inferiority complex,' says the Pentecostal pastor, who saw the light in the mid-1970s, and has waged a holy war against gays ever since. 'I should have won a lot more. I beat myself at different times. This is the truth. If I'd known then what I know now I'd have won six Wimbledons instead of three. I'd have won a lot more tournaments.'

So what does she know now?

It's more about 'who' she knows, I think. 'During a tournament in Paris, I realized that something was missing in my life—a closer relationship with God,' says Court. 'I knew God was there and thought I must be able to know Him in a deeper way … There is so much in the scriptures about the mind. You hear a lot about mental strength in sport. The mind is a battlefield in life whether you're a sports person or a man in the street. It's the gateway down into the heart of man. I wish I'd known it when I was playing instead of thinking about guilt and unworthiness and condemnation. If you change the inside you'll change the outside.'

Anyway, I hope you can make sense of that. What doesn't make any sense at all is why 'The Arm' is generally at the arse end of most peoples' 'all-time greatest' lists. People usually put her down at four, five or six, near Chris Evert and Billie Jean King.

In part, it's for the pretty good reason that some of Court's Slams were won in a depleted field. A few were before 1968, the beginning of the Open Era. And no fewer than eleven were Australian Opens, at a time when most players shunned the tournament. The likes of Virginia Wade, Nancy Richey, and Maria Bueno never made the trip to Australia, and Billie Jean King only came once or twice. Oftentimes the women's side of the draw had just thirty-two players.

But most of Margaret's lowly status probably owes something to her being shy. She played at a time when brash Americans began to dominate the sport and hog the headlines every chance they could get.

These days, however, she *does* get a few headlines, as self-appointed crusader against 'sin'. Victims of homophobia would be better off if she could get some of that pre-God shyness back.

Nicknames: 'The Arm', 'The Aussie Amazon', 'That massive homophobe'

Nationality: Australian

Date of birth: 16 July 1942

Strengths: Serve, volleys, power, speed

Weakness: Slightly to the right of Ghengis Khan

Grand Slams: Australian Open (1960–66, 1969–1971, 1973)
French Open (1962, 1964, 1969–70, 1973)
Wimbledon (1963, 1965, 1970)
US Open (1962, 1965, 1969, 1970, 1973)

In her own words: 'I don't think the younger people today really know what I have done. Personally it doesn't affect me. It is probably a bit sad for the history of the game. But I am not upset about it.'

In somebody else's: 'For sheer strength of performance and accomplishment there has never been a tennis player to match her.' *International Tennis Hall of Fame*

Billie Jean King

For Margaret Court's greatest rival, tennis could be more than a sport. As far as Billie Jean King was concerned, the game played well was actually 'an art form' — a spectacle that is 'capable of moving the players and the audience ... in almost sensual ways'.

'I'm a perfectionist much more than I'm a super competitor,' said the small-statured serve-volleyer, 'and there's a big difference there ... I've been painted as a person who only competes ... But most of all, I get off on hitting a shot correctly ... My heart pounds, my eyes get damp, and my ears feel like they're wiggling, but it's also just totally peaceful. It's almost like having an orgasm.'

Actually, no: 'It's exactly like that.'

You'll be glad to hear that Billie J had plenty of orgasms throughout her illustrious career. It featured twelve Grand Slam singles titles, five years at number one, and far more 'correctly hit' orgasm-causers than there are grains of sand on a beach. King was arguably the best volleyer in the history of tennis: her game was all about speed and placement — and, wherever possible, attacking the net. If Court was the 'Aussie Amazon', Billie Jean was a swarm of bees. Wherever the ball went, she'd be there, and sooner or later you'd get badly stung.

It was an aggressive style that served her well in the most memorable match of her career. For all her great games against Court — and, as she entered her thirties, Navratilova and Evert — it is for the time that she took on a man that BJK is best-known today. Soon to be a Hollywood movie (starring Will Ferrell, if reports are true), the 'Battle of the Sexes' took place in Texas in 1973 in front of 30,000 spectators ... and an estimated TV audience of 50 million.

The exhibition match was prompted by some public comments by a fifty-five-year-old former Wimbledon champ, Bobby Riggs, to the effect that women players were, well, crap. 'Women belong in the bedroom and kitchen, in that order,' said the self-proclaimed 'male chauvinist pig'. And, in many men's eyes, he then managed to prove it, by challenging and beating Margaret Court.

Following that win, Riggs was keen to take on the twenty-nine-year-old King, who was at that time the world number one female player. 'I thought it would set us back 50 years if I didn't win that match,' BJK later said—but on that score she had no problems at all. King ran Riggs ragged in three ripping sets, taking him out 6–4, 6–3, 6–3. 'Most important perhaps for women everywhere, she convinced sceptics that a female athlete can survive pressure-filled situations and that men are as susceptible to nerves as women,' as Neil Amdur wrote the next day in *The New York Times*.

And that certainly wasn't the last blow that King struck for the women's movement. A big personality in a petite body, BJK was tennis's 'first real female firebrand—the first one to throw tantrums and work the media, and demand, loudly, that women should get paid as much as the men'. It was King who launched the Virginia Slims Tour, the first genuinely profitable women's circuit. And it was King who founded the Women's Tennis Association, the female game's governing body to this very day. 'She was a crusader fighting a battle for all of us,' says Martina Navratilova. 'She was carrying the flag; it was all right [for a girl] to be a jock.'

Or gay, for that matter. One of *Life* magazine's '100 Most Important Americans of the 20th Century', and a recent recipient of the Presidential Medal of Freedom, King became a leader in the gay rights movement back when that was unfashionable, after a magazine decided to 'out' her in 1981.

'She has prominently affected the way 50 per cent of society thinks and feels about itself in the vast area of physical exercise,' Frank Deford wrote in *Sports Illustrated*. 'Moreover, like [Arnold] Palmer, she has made a whole sports boom because of the singular force of her presence.'

And, lest we forget, she hit some very good shots.

Chris Evert

Once upon a time, a minor player came face to face with a champion—and was, of course, comprehensively thrashed. 'Thank God my happiness doesn't depend on a tennis match,' quipped Paula Smith in the locker room later. 'Thank God mine does,' Chris Evert replied.

Tennis had never had a competitor like Chris Evert—a woman who had a winning record of over 90 per cent, and so must have been happy for most of the time. In a twenty-year career that began with a US Open semi at sixteen, she clocked up an extraordinary 1304 victories, with just 146 defeats. Only once did Evert fail to reach the semifinals of a Grand Slam, and not once in twelve straight years did she ever leave the top two.

She never tanked, she never had a bad game, she barely even hit double-faults. Like a dog with a bone, Evert clung to every point. And like a dog without a bone, she could bite.

'The way I took losing was probably not really normal,' says the eighteen-time Grand Slam champion, who describes her younger self as 'a therapist's dream'. 'For a while, winning and losing was part of my identity and how I felt about myself, which isn't the healthiest way to feel. It's not really a normal way to grow up knowing that every day, at the end of the day, you're either a winner or a loser and the whole world is writing about you.'

All very true, of course, but had this daughter of a Florida tennis pro been better adjusted, it's unlikely that she'd be in this book. A woman of average height and average strength, with no volley and not much of a serve, Evert built her game around groundstrokes that were ... well ... fairly solid. Her two-handed backhand had precision and depth and spin, but it wasn't much chop compared to Evonne Goolagong's. And while her forehand was a model of consistency, it wasn't exactly a weapon compared to Marita Redondo's.

But Evert won many more Grand Slams than Goolagong. And she ravaged Redondo every time they met. The 'therapist's dream' became a nightmare for all her opponents because she put simply *everything* into every single point. Described by one writer as 'a neurological miracle'—and nicknamed 'the Ice Maiden' by everyone else—Evert never showed any emotion on court, whatever the circumstances and whatever the stakes. She never disputed a line call, however egregious, and she never made an error on a crucial point. When the stakes rose, so did her standard: the Ice Maiden never melted under pressure; in fact, that's when she fired.

'She concentrates to the last point,' is how Margaret Court put it. 'It makes her a champion. Even when she is losing, she concentrates and doesn't give up.'

'There are players who are stronger than Evert and more naturally talented athletes than Evert and more explosive volleyers than Evert,' wrote a *Sports Illustrated* journalist in 1975. 'What Evert has more of, what makes her a champion who each year moves farther and farther beyond the reach of mortal tennis players, is grit. Chris Evert has true grit. Character. Mental tenacity. She is a clear thinker in a thoughtful game. And she never gives up.'

And America loved her for it. Blonde, tanned and girl-next-doory, Evert was the pretty face (and if we're honest, the sexy legs, too) of women's tennis throughout the 1970s. You could even see it on every breakfast table, underneath the words 'Breakfast of Champions' on boxes of Wheaties.

But Chris Evert didn't eat Wheaties. She ate pressure for breakfast, and then she had some for lunch.

Martina Navratilova

Nowadays, power tennis is commonplace. With bouncy modern balls, speedy modern courts and racquets made of God-knows-what, we're all used to seeing shots whoosh by in a blink of an eye and then whoosh back even faster than that.

But back in the BG era—that is to say, before graphite—it was still possible to see power tennis: you just had to check out a certain Czech. Martina Navratilova may have had a wooden racquet but, the way that she was able to whack the ball, it may as well have been a big wooden club.

'Martina revolutionised the game by her superb athleticism and aggressiveness,' says Chris Evert of the player who spent more time in the gym than any woman before her—and, quite possibly, any woman since. 'She brought athleticism to a whole new level with her training techniques—particularly cross-training, the idea that you could go to the gym or play basketball to get in shape for tennis. She had everything down to a science, including her diet.'

But Martina was far from an automaton: her game had dash and style. Fond of chipping and charging to the net, when common sense clearly said to stay back, she was an aggressive, emotional serve-volleyer, whose matches had plenty of ups and downs.

Mostly, though, they had ups. The winner of 329 singles and doubles titles—far more than any other player, male or female—Martina collected no fewer than fifty-six Grand Slam titles, eighteen of them in singles, in a career that spanned four decades. With Margaret Court and the 1940s player Doris Hart, she is one of just three players to have won every single Slam in singles, women's doubles, and mixed doubles (a feat that some call the career 'boxed set').

But for all the Czech-turned-American's extraordinary wins, it took her a long time to win over the crowds. As sportswriter Frank Deford put it, Martina was always 'the other, the odd one, alone: left-hander in a right-handed universe, gay in a straight world; defector, immigrant; the (last?) gallant volleyer among all those duplicate baseline bytes. When she came into the game, she was the European among Americans; she leaves as the American among Europeans—and the only grown-up left in the tennis crib. Can't she ever get it right?'

Well, no. Being born behind the Iron Curtain was no way to win over Reagan's America: baby Martina should have planned ahead. But she always found homophobia a bigger issue than xenophobia. Navratilova's willingness to come out of the closet, rather than stay in (or, indeed, commit suicide), cost her millions in commercial endorsements, and earned her some frosty receptions from crowds. 'It was tough,' says the first sporting superstar to have actually come out of the closet at the top of their game. 'If I complained about a line call, ooh they got on my case immediately. It didn't take much.'

The media, too, didn't exactly cover itself in glory after Navratilova confirmed 'all the lesbian rumours' in 1981. 'I couldn't lie, but it led to some very demeaning articles. They wrote that I would pick my doubles partner so I could look at her bum when I was serving and she was at the net, that kind of stuff . . . I didn't fit on so many levels. I came from a Communist country, I had an aggressive playing style, and on top of that I was gay, while Chris was the perfect girl-next-door. There couldn't have been a greater contrast, in fact before we played a final in Florida once one paper wrote it up as good versus evil. That was the headline: "Good versus evil".'

Luckily, however, evil eventually triumphed: Martina is now a much-loved international icon who finally gets the love she deserves. 'Martina is probably the most daring player in the history of the game,' said legendary TV analyst Bud Collins when Navratilova finally retired. 'She dared to play a style antithetical to her heritage without worrying about making a fool of herself. She dared to remake herself physically, setting new horizons for women in sports. And she dared to live her life as she chose, without worrying what other people thought of her.'

And, dare I say it, she's also the best of all time.

Steffi Graf

In October 1982, world number two Tracy Austin flew to Stuttgart to play in the Porsche Grand Prix. Her first-round opponent was a little blonde girl with a very big forehand, who had travelled from nearby Mannheim to play her first pro tournament. Just thirteen years old, she was the second-youngest player ever to earn an international ranking—and far from the only player that Austin thrashed that year. The American champ was less than impressed by the 'prodigy', however, afterwards telling reporters that there were 'hundreds like her' back home.

Incorrect. Women's tennis had never seen a player like Steffi Graf. It had seen steady baseliners like Wills and Evert, and attacking serve-volleyers like Martina and Margaret, but never before had it seen a player who could unleash winners from the back of the court again and again and again. Steffi Graf was a capable volleyer and a powerful server, and she had a rather nice backhand slice. But it was not for nothing that she was nicknamed 'Fraulein Forehand'. The best shot in the history of women's tennis, Graf's forehand was a whiplash that could wipe out an opponent before a proper rally had even begun.

Mind you, Steffi certainly could rally when she needed to: speed was another one of her strengths. At the 1988 Olympics she ran with some German athletes, 'just for fun', and clocked a time that could have put her in the 800-metre final.

As it happens, she won a gold medal that year anyway—taking the women's singles title, along with the four majors, to achieve tennis's first ever 'Golden Grand Slam'. That year was the highlight of an already glittering career, which saw her collect seven Wimbledons, five US Opens, six French Opens and four Australian Opens, and spend a record-breaking 377 weeks as world number one.

Though 1989 wasn't too bad either. Graf fell just one game short of a second Grand Slam that year, and also managed to win sixty-six matches in a row. It's still the second-longest-ever winning streak in the history of the women's game.

Was any player ever better than Steffi Graf in the late 1980s? Possibly not, but there have been ones who were happier. Not all that unusually for a tennis prodigy, Graf grew up with a dictator in the place of a dad. Eventually jailed for tax evasion, Peter Graf gave Steffi her first racquet when she was three years old, and told her she could have ice-cream whenever she managed to hit a ball back to him at least twenty-five times in a row. 'Most of the time, on the 25th ball, I would hit it too hard or so she could not return it, because you cannot have ice cream all the time.'

And you can't have fun all the time, either. Already shy by nature, Steffi was often not allowed to go to parties, because she was too busy practising—and she would sometimes get 'a good smacking' if she didn't perfect a new shot.

Now very happily retired, Steffi today goes by the name of Stephanie and runs a charity for children who've been scarred by war. She rarely watches, let alone attends, a tennis match—and describes her tennis career as something 'very much in the past'.

'I never hanker after the past,' she said in a rare interview. 'I prefer to devote myself to new tasks. The last few years in particular have gone like the wind. Recently they showed French Open Classics on TV here—the high points from past tournaments. I don't really enjoy seeing myself on the court, but this time I did watch for a few minutes. Andre told the children, "Look, that's Mom playing." Then he asked me, "What was the final result?" I racked my brains, but couldn't remember.'

'Andre' is, of course, Andre Agassi, Graf's husband and fellow former star. And a man whose own father rigged up a machine when he was seven ... that was designed to shoot balls at his body at 110 miles per hour.

The couple live with their two children in a sprawling Las Vegas mansion. It does not have a tennis court.

Serena Williams

The name Serena is derived from *serenus*, a Latin word meaning tranquil and serene.

The player Serena is derived from the Williams family of Compton, Los Angeles, and she's not serene at all. Famous for her colourful outfits on the court, and a couple of see-through ones off it, 'ReRe' is always happy to wear her heart on her sleeve—or, better still, talk with her mouth. She's described tennis officials as 'white losers' and 'honkies' over the years, and quite a few people that she's lost to as 'lucky'.

Serena herself, on the other hand, is 'a global icon'. 'I'm an actress, model and athlete, and I'd put athlete third on the list,' says the woman who also regards herself as 'an unbelievable designer'.

Let's at least agree that she's an unbelievable tennis player. With far and away the best serve in the history of women's tennis, and a crunching forehand that probably belongs in the top five, Williams has simply been able to outmuscle finesse-merchants like Martina Hingis, a girl who looked like being an all-time great until the big-hitting Serena appeared on the scene.

'When historians of the future look back on the women's game, they will most certainly point to one event that changed the course of the game more significantly than any other,' says sportswriter JA Allen. 'When the Williams sisters emerged in the late 1990s as teenagers, the women's game changed forever. The serve became more than getting play underway, it became a weapon—the underpinning of the new power game in women's tennis.'

Tennis had seen powerful women before, of course, from Wills, to Court, to Graf. But they'd always coexisted with the consistent and the crafty. Nowadays, everyone's a baseliner, and lobs, slices and chips are a thing of the past. If you want to beat Serena Williams, it has to be at her own game, but that's a lot easier said than done.

There have been three distinct Serena eras since she and her sister first emerged from Compton, an impoverished sprawl of gangs, guns and drugs in the southern part of downtown LA. The first was from 1999 to 2003, when she won six Grand Slam titles ... and wore outfits ranging from a black Lycra catsuit to a short denim skirt with thigh-high boots.

The following five years saw Serena battle injury and depression, and struggle to stay interested in the game. She didn't play too many tournaments until 2008, but still managed to snare two Grand Slams.

And since the Wimbledon of that year, we've had Super Serena. Nine-More-Grand-Slams Serena. The Serena who some say is the best of all time.

'She's the greatest tennis player that we've ever seen up until this point,' said Chris Evert. 'Maybe 20 years from now somebody else will come out but [right now] nobody has ever had the power and the shots and the serve and the complete package that she has. If she plays for another three years, if she wins one or two [majors per year] she could very well pass Steffi [Graf's total of twenty-two Slams]. The key to her game is just staying healthy and being fit and just being interested and inspired. This is peak Serena.'

So sit back and enjoy the show.

Nicknames: 'ReRe', 'Momma Smash'

Nationality: American

Date of birth: 26 September 1981

Strengths: Power, serve, groundstrokes

Weakness: Her personality

Grand Slams: Australian Open (2003, 2005, 2007, 2009–10)
    French Open (2002, 2013)
    Wimbledon (2002–03, 2009–10, 2012)
    US Open (1999, 2002, 2008, 2012–14)

In her own words: 'I am a global icon.'

In somebody else's: 'I think she's the greatest tennis player that we've ever seen up until this point.' *Chris Evert*

6

THE GRAND RIVALRIES

From Coke versus Pepsi to Stalin versus Trotsky, history is full of great rivalries. But how many of them involved great tennis? About eight, I'd say.

Rod Laver versus Ken Rosewall

With twenty-eight Davis Cups to its credit, not to mention its very own Slam, Australia is without a doubt one of the great tennis nations. But it's also true to say that we're not very good. The past thirty-five years have netted Australia's finest players precisely seven Grand Slam titles, out of a possible total of 280. That's a winning percentage of 0.35 per cent. Or to use the technical term: bugger all.

Things were a little different back in the 1950s, when our men and women collected twenty-two cups. And the 1960s weren't too bad, either: in that decade, we won fifty. With the likes of Tony Roche, John Newcombe and Roy Emerson carving up the court—not to mention Evonne Goolagong and, of course, Mrs Court —Australia truly was a tennis powerhouse, rather than the outhouse that we are today.

But of all the stars in that golden era, no-one shone more brightly than a short, slow redhead from Rockhampton and an even shorter guy who was built like a twig. 'Rocket' Rod Laver and Ken 'Muscles' Rosewall may not have *looked* like great tennis players but they certainly played like them. The latter won eight Grand Slam titles over a three-decade career that was largely spent not playing Slams at all.

But it was on the (pre-1968) pro tour that fans saw the best of Rosewall, a Sydney boy whose sliced backhand could cut opponents to ribbons, and then cut each of those ribbons into long, slender threads. Generally considered the second-best backhand in history (behind the brutal baseball shot belonging to Don Budge), it was a much harder, faster and more versatile shot than the defensive slice mostly in use today. Muscles didn't just use his slice for those occasions when he wanted to approach the net. He used it to lob and to rally and to return serve—and, above all, to hit lots of winners.

We'll never know how many winners Muscles would have hit against his great mate Laver—and we'll never know how many matches either man won. 'We don't know how many times we played,' says Rocket of his epic rivalry with the man he calls the 'least appreciated great player in the history of tennis'—a rivalry which was played out over at least 100 matches on the pre–Open Era professional circuit. 'Nobody was counting.'

But plenty of people were watching. 'Some people said those one-nighters were nothing but exhibitions, which annoyed us,' said Frank Sedgman, 'but I'll tell you, Rocket and Kenny gave everything every time they played. They were both great competitors.'

> **Laver versus Rosewall (1963–1976)**
> **All matches:** Laver 80–64
> **All finals:** Laver 36–20
> **Grand Slam matches:** 1–1
> * Figures exclude indefinite number of exhibition matches

Björn Borg versus John McEnroe

Ali versus Frazier. Senna versus Prost. Rangers versus Celtic. America versus good taste. The world is full of great rivalries. And where tennis racquets are involved, none of them beat that between John McEnroe and Björn Borg—a four-year tussle between two towering talents for the top spot on the tennis tree.

Ok, all out of T-words now. Terribly sorry.

What made Borg–McEnroe matches so special to watch was the dramatic contrast in their temperaments and styles. It was right-hander versus left-hander and baseliner versus serve-volleyer; soft-spoken Swede versus crass, loud New Yorker. It was tortured genius versus streamlined efficiency. It was an artist raging against the machine. HBO recently released a documentary about pair's twenty-two-match rivalry which some executive decided to call *Fire and Ice*. If you ask me (as yet, nobody has), that title pretty much sums it all up.

Borg was the first to turn pro. He won five Slams between 1973 and 1978, the year that the Big Mac finally arrived on the scene. In the four years that followed, until his sudden retirement in the early eighties, Borg collected another six of them—but Mac himself managed to win four. The pair's dominance of the Grand Slam circuit during that four-year period is all the more astonishing when you consider that neither man even bothered to enter the Australian Open, that tournament just being too far away.

But for all their dominance of the majors, Borg and McEnroe never managed to dominate each other. They met fourteen times—and in four Grand Slam finals—and won exactly seven matches apiece. Their 1981 Wimbledon final, with that famously long four-set tie breaker, is still talked about as the best tennis match of all time, and many say that Borg's loss to the rising American star was what led him to abandon the game.

But that rising star never soared quite as high as he might have: McEnroe never won another major after 1984. 'I don't think people understand it was a James Dean type of rivalry—it came and went,' says tennis writer Mary Carillo. 'And McEnroe never had another rival that made him aspire.'

> **Borg versus McEnroe (1978–1981)**
> All matches: 7–7
> All finals: McEnroe 5–4
> Grand Slam matches: McEnroe 3–1

Martina Navratilova versus Chris Evert

'I was always the visiting team,' said Martina Navratilova of her famous rivalry against Chris Evert—an eighty-match, eleven-year epic which Middle America tended to see in terms of evil and good. 'She was the American girl-next-door and here I am, this big muscular lesbian from a communist country. I came up against the Osmonds of tennis.'

But even if you were to take all the red-baiting and gay-hating out of the equation, you *could* kind of see what they meant: Martina was, after all, so very, very big, and the 5'6", 56 kg Evert was so comparatively small. It's just a human instinct to support David, even if it turns out that Goliath's quite nice.

But what if David is a bit of a prick? While Martina was actually quite an emotional player, and not immune to teary breakdowns on court, Evert's pert, dainty blondeness actually hid the heart of a ruthless jock. 'We were night and day,' said Evert, whose remorseless pursuit of victory won her eighteen Slams but not too many friends on the tour. 'People would [come up to me and say,] "You know, I never liked that Martina. She's so tough." I'd say, "You know what? She's a kitten. She really is. I'm the hard one." They'd say, "No, no, no—not you. You're so frail and feminine; we always felt sorry for you." It was as if Martina became the bully to some people. And I was the person who could silence the bully.'

It was at least true that Evert could *beat* her. Three years older than the rising Czech star, she was already a three-Slam winner when Martina joined the pro tour in 1975—and by 1977, Evert was a seven-Slam winner, and indisputably the best player in the world. Her dominance prompted the overweight and not exactly overcommitted Martina to change her diet and hit the gym. And the results quickly changed as well.

After winning just five of their first twenty-five matches, Navratilova finished up 43–37 ahead.

All together those numbers add up to eighty matches over eleven years. Eighty matches played almost exclusively in semifinals and finals. And eleven years in which one of the two was always ranked number one. Between 1978 and 1986, they together won twenty-five of the twenty-eight Grand Slams they entered. The surprisingly close friends didn't just dominate women's tennis. They *were* women's tennis.

'We brought out the best in each other,' Navratilova once said. 'It's almost not right to say who's better. If you tried to make the perfect rivalry, we were it.'

> **Evert versus Navratilova (1973–1988)**
> All matches: Navratilova 43–37
> All finals: Navratilova 36–25
> Grand Slam matches: Navratilova 14–8

Stefan Edberg versus Boris Becker

Some rivalries are infused by hatred. Others, unfortunately, are not.

'Boris has been very good for my tennis and I hope I have been good for his,' said the serve-volleying Swede Stefan Edberg, of the man he played some thirty-five times. 'We were actually quite close,' agreed Becker, man enough to accept his fair share of the blame. 'There was always tremendous respect [and] never any bad blood, which was astonishing given how many big finals we played. It was never personal, just the tennis.'

Perhaps one reason why the rivalry was never really personal was that Edberg never really had a personality. About as charismatic as an undertaker with a nasty cold, but far less likely to laugh, joke or smile, Edberg could produce smooth groundstrokes, crisp volleys and clever kick serves—but for all that, he never put on a show. 'I was reserved and introverted,' is how the six-time Grand Slam winner now explains it. 'Boris was the exact opposite: irascible and emotional.'

Yes he was, God bless him. The blue-eyed, strawberry-blond 'Boom Boom' electrified the tennis world when he won the Wimbledon final as an unseeded seventeen-year-old, with a game based on power and athleticism. (And diving volleys. And a ridiculously big serve). Constantly muttering and grumbling to himself, like a man on the verge of a nervous breakdown, Becker based his game entirely on emotion. And when you were watching him play out there, it was pretty hard not to feel it as well.

Also a six-time Grand Slam winner, Becker eventually made a habit of appearing in Wimbledon finals—and in 1988, 1989 and 1990, he faced Edberg in three in a row. The Swedish star snared two of them, but the German player ended up ahead in their overall meetings, winning twenty-five games to ten.

Their lives ever since have followed predictable paths—Edberg to a quiet suburban existence; Becker to headlines and broom cupboards—but in recent years, those paths have rejoined. Becker has become Novak Djokovic's new coach. Edberg is now helping out Federer. It's a chance to renew their rivalry—and that's a chance that neither man wants to miss.

Game on.

> **Edberg versus Becker (1984–1996)**
> All matches: Becker 25–10
> All finals: Becker 14–5
> Grand Slam matches: Edberg 3–1

Steffi Graf versus Monica Seles

Tennis has had many intense rivalries—but only one of them has actually seen blood spilt. On 30 April 1993, the world's number one player, Monica Seles, was stabbed by a crazed fan of the world's number two, the slightly older and more established Steffi Graf. Fortunately, the wound was just an inch or so deep, and confined to the shoulder blade (rather than, say, her spine). Physically, the Serbian star just took a few weeks to recover, but psychologically, she probably still hasn't. 'I was plunged into a fog of darkness and depression that I couldn't see my way out of,' Seles wrote in a newspaper article sixteen years later.

Perhaps the saddest thing about the attack was that it was entirely successful. Günter Parche achieved his goal of getting Graf back to world number one. Seles lost motivation after the incident, developed a mild eating disorder and 'started finding excuses for avoiding the treadmill. Even 10 minutes of walking was torture … Darkness had descended into my head.' She was never quite the same player when she finally returned to the court two years later, and we'll never know what she might have achieved.

Mind you, she'd achieved quite a bit already. In 1990, when sixteen-year-old Seles began her career, Graf essentially had no rival at all. The German had been the best player in the world since 1987 and in that time easily snaffled nine Slams. But the shrieking Serbian soon changed all that: with a double-handed forehand that was powerful enough to kill a man, and a grunt that was loud enough to bring him right back to life, Monica Seles won eight Grand Slams from 1990 to 1993—the three years that it took her to turn twenty. It was quite simply a reign of terror.

After Seles's stabbing, Graf quickly regained the top spot, and she didn't relinquish it for a number of years. But should it have been Graf's to begin with? Can we really call her the greatest player of all time when she might not even have been the best in her own time?

Who knows? All we can say is that the German actually led Seles 10–5 in their head-to-head encounters. And it would have been nice to see them play even more.

> **Graf versus Seles (1989–1999)**
> All matches: Graf 10–5
> All finals: Graf 6–4
> Grand Slam matches: Graf 6–4

Andre Agassi versus Pete Sampras

Time heals all wounds. Unless you're Andre Agassi and Pete Sampras.

The two best players of the 1990s but never the best of friends, the baseliner and the serve-volleyer recently came together to play a charity event. And then nearly came to blows. 'Hit for Haiti was unfortunate,' Agassi later said of the fundraiser, which saw the two players exchange insults in front of a TV camera, with big, fat microphones in hand. 'I've since apologised.'

He may also need to apologise for his 2009 autobiography, which described his long-time rival Sampras as 'dull', 'uninspiring,' and 'more robotic than a parrot.' (And just to round out the portrait, a really bad tipper.) 'Our relationship is strictly platonic,' Agassi wrote. 'As much time as we spent together, I never really knew him. Two different people, two different styles. Those differences were never bridged between us. But I recognise him as a superior athlete.'

So does almost everyone else. While Agassi—a counter-puncher with cat-like reflexes, whose return of serve was like a nuclear bomb—won Slams on all four surfaces, he finished his career with 'only' eight. Sampras, on the other hand, won fourteen of the suckers, a figure which easily makes him an all-time great.

But Sampras was never greater than when he was playing the US-born son of an Iranian boxer—a man who could hit almost anything back over the net. The pair met in five Grand Slam finals, with Sampras winning four. Pistol Pete also ended up comfortably ahead in their overall matches (20–14), but there was never was anything very comfortable about the matches themselves. With Sampras's smooth, classical serve and volley game a perfect foil for Agassi's crunching groundstrokes, they presented a delicious contrast in styles, as well as personalities (Agassi being the Las Vegas Showman, Sampras the Californian Bore). It was possibly the best serve of all time versus arguably the best return of serve of all time, and the result was definitely some of history's best points.

As Agassi put it a little while ago, 'The excitement and intensity between Pete and me is way beyond anything I experience playing the other guys. He's the one guy I feel gives me no say in the match. Just knowing he's out there inspires me.'

'It's special playing Andre,' agreed Sampras. 'He's the one guy who, even if I'm playing well, can take me down. But I think we both hope the other reaches the finals in all the Slams. That's what this is all about. To go down in history as one of the great rivalries in tennis ... that would be the ultimate.'

> **Agassi versus Sampras (1989–2002)**
> All matches: Sampras 20–14
> All finals: Sampras 9–7
> Grand Slam matches: Sampras 6–3

Serena Williams versus Venus Williams

It is, as a journalist once put it, 'a scenario as improbable as one set of parents raising Picasso and Monet.' Hundreds of millions of female tennis players in the world, and two of the best-ever share the same DNA.

Both world number ones at various stages in their careers—Venus for just eleven weeks, Serena for 200 and counting—the Williams sisters have won some twenty-three Grand Slams between them. Not to mention another thirteen playing doubles together, a hobby that has also netted them three Olympic gold medals. All in all, it's not a bad record for two kids from Compton, Los Angeles—a part of the world best known for gang warfare, not to mention poverty and crime and drugs.

But for all the tennis miracles that they've managed to accomplish, the Williams sisters' greatest achievement may be their sisterly bond. These are two people who spent their first two decades living together, and also training together six hours a day, six days a week. They shared the same bedroom and they competed in the same tournaments. You would expect them to hate, or at the very least annoy, each other, but instead they're the closest of friends.

Indeed, it's this friendship that makes the sisters' rivalry so fascinating—because it often seems like there's no rivalry at all. Games between the pair have historically been awkward, prodding, passionless affairs, with neither woman really playing her best. Early on in their careers, their father Richard was even accused of 'fixing' the results, and some conspiracy theorists insist he still does.

> **Williams versus Williams (1998–2014)**
> All matches: Serena 14–11
> All finals: Serena 8–3
> Grand Slam matches: Serena 7–5

The real explanation is a whole lot more simple: no-one likes to see their loved ones lose. 'I don't exactly feel like I've won,' says Venus of her increasingly rare victories over her little sister (she trails 11–14 overall). 'I just hate to see Serena lose, even against me. I'm the big sister. I make sure she has everything, even if I don't have anything. I love her and it's hard.'

'I don't love playing her,' agrees Serena. 'If I win, I'm not super excited, and if I lose I'm really not excited.'

Speak for yourself, Serena. Sister versus sister is psychodrama par excellence.

Roger Federer versus Rafael Nadal

Federer and Nadal are two of the greatest players of all time. But do they really have a great rivalry?

Chris Evert says yes. 'I would say Federer is more like an artist, and Nadal is a warrior. Different styles, different temperaments, different personalities. That's what makes a great rivalry.'

But the actual statistics say no. Put Vincent van Gogh in the ring with Attila the Hun, and the results could get pretty ugly. Equally, there's a case to be made that the most celebrated rivalry of modern times isn't even a rivalry at all: Nadal simply keeps on slaughtering the guy. The record between the Spaniard and the Swiss stands at 23–10, with Nadal leading 9–2 in Grand Slams.

Some people say that this lopsided record just comes down to happenstance: Federer's weakest shot—his right-handed backhand—happens to be right in the firing line of Nadal's best shot, his left-handed, crosscourt forehand. It's certainly true that the Spaniard is a bad match-up for the Swiss. But it may also be true to say that he's simply better.

But whatever the story, there's no doubt that they're fun to watch. The pair's 2008 Wimbledon final—a titanic 6–4 6–4 6–7 6–7 9–7 Nadal victory—is widely regarded as one of the best matches in history, while the five-set final that they played the year before that was also pretty damn good to watch. Nadal versus Federer matches are lefty versus righty and clay-courter versus all-courter. They are youth versus age and power versus grace. They are a bucket full of sweatiness versus godlike serenity.

And, lest we forget, they're a meeting of mates. Throughout all their time at the top of the tree (and they were world number one and two for five consecutive years), the pair have somehow managed to remain reasonably chummy. *Reasonably* chummy ...

'We're almost too nice to each other sometimes,' Federer recently admitted, in a rare breach of the diplomatic facade. 'I don't want to say today's players are too soft, but it's good when players go after each other a bit. I'm not sure how close we are as friends. I'll be interested how much we'll stay in touch once everything is said and done and we're off the circuit. We're not going to dinner, if you know what I mean.'

Yes, Roger, I think we do.

> **Federer versus Nadal (2004–2014)**
> All matches: Nadal 23–10
> All finals: Nadal 14–6
> Grand Slam matches: Nadal 9–2

7

THE GRAND GAMES

Is there anything better than a truly great game of tennis? (Well, apart from sex, obviously. And drugs can sometimes be good. We also shouldn't forget the joy of a good book or movie, and there's certainly something very nice about dinner with your family and friends.)

Anyway, if we can put aside all of that stuff (and scuba diving as well, come to think of it—it's great, you should give it a go), please believe me when I tell you that *nothing* beats watching a great game of tennis. Here are eight that you might have missed.

Henri Cochet versus Bill Tilden
Wimbledon semifinal, 1927

Henri Cochet was a *très bon* tennis player—*un amateur de sport* with plenty of panache, not to mention esprit and elan. One of France's Four Musketeers—the four Frenchmen who dominated the game in the late twenties and early thirties—Cochet was a jaunty little fellow with a nice big smile. He widely known as 'the Wizard' thanks to his tricky half-volleys and fondness for strange angles and slightly odd shots.

But like all wizards, he sometimes had off days, where the muse just went AWOL for no reason. 'Henri Cochet can beat everybody when his shots are working,' his fellow Musketeer René Lacoste once said, 'and he can be beaten by everybody when they are not.'

Cochet's famous Wimbledon semifinal started out like one of the latter type of days. Up against the world's number one player, Big Bill Tilden, the Frenchman very quickly began to go down. In almost no time at all, the score was 6–2, 6–4, 5–1. With his brutal power and blistering serves, Tilden wasn't beating the little Frenchman so much as *bullying* him: it was like watching a man play a boy.

But then the boy grew up. When he suddenly found himself three points from defeat, Cochet evidently decided that he had nothing to lose. The Frenchman started to go for a winner on virtually every single shot—and somehow managed to hit seventeen in a row. Six straight games later, Cochet had won the third set. Two hours later, he'd won the match.

Vive la France!

'Pancho' Gonzales versus Charlie Pasarell
Wimbledon first round, 1969

'Always two there are,' said Yoda, the Jedi master who never quite mastered English. 'A master and an apprentice.'

At the All England Championships of 1969, the master was Mr Ricardo 'Pancho' Gonzales. A grey-haired forty-one-year-old superstar, who had spent the previous two decades on the professional tour after abandoning his amateur status at age twenty-one. That had still given him enough time to pick up two Grand Slams, however—and with Wimbledon now open to both amateurs and professionals, Pancho was very keen to pick up a third. The fiery competitor hadn't played his best tennis for at least a decade, or tennis of *any* description for at least a couple of months, but he was the kind of player you'd write off at your peril. (For one thing, he'd probably yell at you.)

The apprentice was Charlie Pasarell. A one-time child star who Gonzales had once coached, and who he now had to face in the first round. In 1968, the twenty-five-year-old Pasarell's career had yet to really live up to expectations. But you would expect him to be in better shape than a forty-one-year-old.

And you'd be perfectly right. These were the days before tie breaks, and before players were allowed sit down during changes of ends. These were the days before players could get treated by physios, or stop the game for a quick massage. Most commentators felt that if this match lasted any more than three sets, Passarell's youth would likely give him the edge.

The now famous clash between the two began on a gloomy Tuesday evening at the unusually late time of 6 pm. Rain had washed out the previous day's play, so officials felt that they had no choice but to try and squeeze the match in—and once it had started, people had no choice but to watch. The first set was the longest in Wimbledon history, and very probably one of the best. Pasarell chipped and lobbed and ran the ageing warrior off his feet; Pancho served aces, smashed lobs, and snarled. The set went serve for serve for forty-five games, until Pasarell finally snared a break in the forty-sixth, and closed it out, 24–22.

By now it was almost 8 pm, and daylight was fading fast. Gonzales, whose eyesight had never been great, said that play needed to be abandoned. And he became *furious* when the umpire said no. The next set was one long tantrum—or, rather, one short one, because Pancho lost it 6–1. Spectators say that he effectively threw all six games away, having spent most of them swearing and shouting, and repeatedly demanding that the umpire halt play. When he finally did, Pancho hurled a racquet at the base of his chair, and stormed off to the jeers of the crowd.

That night, Passarell had a quiet dinner, and went to bed for a good long sleep.

Pancho, on the other hand, stayed up until 2 am, playing backgammon with an old flame.

It was sunny when play resumed on Wednesday morning, and the game itself was simply red-hot. Gonzales was 'so tired that he could scarcely hold his racquet', and so stricken with cramp that he could hardly move. But he still managed to save seven match points in front of a jam-packed stadium. And finally win over five epic sets.

The final score was 22–24, 1–6, 16–14, 6–3, 11–9—a grand total of 112 games.

Billie Jean King versus Margaret Court
Wimbledon final, 1970

Everybody likes a friendly rivalry, but an unfriendly one is better still. The two dominant players of the sixties and seventies, Margaret Court and Billie Jean King, hated each other in such a heartfelt way that close observers found it rather uplifting. 'Margaret represents everything Billie Jean hates, and Billie Jean represents everything Margaret despises,' says Peachy Kellmeyer, the WTA vice president.

And, despite that God-awful nickname, Peachy's got it in one. Court was a quiet, shy and deeply conservative person—and when I say 'conservative', I mean crazily right-wing. The woman basically belongs in the Middle Ages (where, with a bit of luck, she'd die from the plague). Now the pastor of her very own Pentecostal church, and the daughter- and sister-in-law of two Tory premiers, Court is a loud and proud campaigner against gays and abortion—two sinful 'choices' that are 'an abomination to the Lord'.

Billie Jean King, on the other hand, is a gay woman. Who once had an abortion. And is quite loud and progressive. When BJK took Court's number one ranking in 1966, it was never going to be the beginning of a beautiful friendship. The only wonder was that no-one got shot.

The 1970 Wimbledon final arguably saw both players at the peak of their powers: the serve-volleying King right in the middle of her career, the baseliner Court midway through a potential Grand Slam. 'Here were two gloriously gifted players at their best, or so close to it that the margin was irrelevant,' a *Times* journalist enthused the next day. 'They gave us a marvellous blend of athleticism and skill, courage and concentration. They moved each other about with remorseless haste and hit a flashing stream of lovely shots. The match was punctuated throughout by rallies of wondrously varied patterns.'

The first set was the longest ever played in a Wimbledon final, and involved an extraordinary eight breaks of serve. Court finally took it out, 14–12. 'You could hear a pin drop because there was such great tension in there,' the Australian later said of that set—and, with her ankle injury starting to play up, she'd been feeling quite tense herself. 'They told me the injection would last two-and-a-half hours and it was getting pretty close to that, so I thought if it goes to three sets I was going to lose.'

The second set was even *more* dramatic, with King saving no less than five match points. The sixth one, however, she lost—giving Court a 14–12, 11–9 victory, her third win at Wimbledon. And the third leg in her 1968 Grand Slam.

The two women did not embrace at the net.

Michael Chang versus Ivan Lendl
French Open final, 1989

Yes, okay, Ivan Lendl may have looked like a border security guard, but he was a soft, gentle soul underneath. Take the time in 1988 when the dour Czech was due to play an exhibition match against Boris Becker in Iowa. When Becker cancelled at the last minute, organisers needed a replacement—and the only one they could find was a short, skinny sixteen-year-old living not far away, who had only very recently turned pro.

The world's number one player duly crushed Michael Chang, and then took him aside for a fatherly word. 'Do you want to know why I beat you today?' Lendl asked him.

'OK,' Chang said, 'tell me why you kicked my butt so bad.'

'Truthfully, you've got nothing that can hurt me. You've got no serve; your second serve is not very strong. So, pretty much, whenever I play you, I can do whatever I want, however I want, and I'm going to beat you pretty sweet like I did today.'

Now, tell me that that isn't lovely!

Anyway, the next chapter in the story occurred in the fourth round of the next year's French Open. To everyone's vast surprise, the now seventeen-year-old Chang had managed to get to the final of the tournament, and was now facing Old Steely Eyes himself. And to no-one's surprise, the world number one took the first two sets. 'Chang wasn't in his league,' says the iconic tennis journo Bud Collins. 'He's looking at this little guy across the net, thinking, "I won the first two sets, what are you doing here? Go home."'

Chang, however, did not go home. With metronomic consistency and incredible court speed, he instead won the next two sets. With two steady baseliners just slugging away, it may not have been the most varied of tennis matches—but as a David and Goliath–type spectacle, it was up there with, well, um, David and Goliath.

By the fifth set, however, that court speed was taking its toll on Chang. 'I started to cramp anytime I had to run really hard,' he later recalled, 'so I resorted to hitting a lot of [slow, looping] moon balls [to give himself time to recover], and trying to keep points as short as possible. If I had an opportunity to go for a winner, I'd go for it.'

The tactics got Chang to a 4–3 lead, but by that time the cramps had started affecting his serve. 'Every time when I went up for my serve, my legs would cramp [too]. My first serve was going maybe 60 miles an hour—that was it. I was having a more difficult time holding my serve than breaking his. I was really close to quitting,' he said.

Instead, at 15–30, he tried something different. Something remarkable. An underarm serve. Taken aback, Lendl hit an awkward forehand return, which Chang easily dispatched cross-court. 'The crowd went nuts,' said Chang, and 'from there, the whole tide of the match really, really turned … He was kind of going like this [tapping his head] and it became a sort of mental battle.'

A mental battle which Lendl lost. After four hours and thirty-nine minutes, Chang became the youngest male Grand Slam champion in history. It would be the only Grand Slam title of his career.

And to his credit, Lendl became a gracious loser. 'In my mind, that match was not that important,' he recently told ESPN.

Jimmy Connors versus Aaron Krickstein
US Open fourth round, 1991

At the age of thirty-nine, most of us rise out of bed all sore, fat and weary, wishing polite society didn't consider 7 am to be too early to start drinking. Tennis is a sport for young people. As Roger Federer is starting to show us, players very rarely age well.

The one exception seems to be Jimmy Connors. *He* made the US Open semifinals. It was an amazing run for a greying, faintly paunchy wildcard who was ranked 174 in the world. A man who had played just three matches that year due to a wrist injury ... and won none of them.

The blue-collar slugger's first win of the year came against Patrick McEnroe at the first round of the Open—and that win was arguably the greatest of all. Down two sets to nil, 0–3 and love–40, Connors did not exactly get off to the most promising of starts, but somehow he was ahead at the end.

But it was his fourth-round match against Aaron Krickstein that everyone remembers these days, largely because it was the match that everybody actually watched. After his come-from-behind win against McEnroe, and two slay-from-in-front smashings in rounds two and three, Connors's progress through the tournament had become an international news story—attracting unprecedented interest among America's football-loving blue-collar workers, and record TV ratings and ear-splitting crowds. 'It's Jimmy's tournament now, no matter what happens,' said Pete Sampras with perfect accuracy.

Sometimes described as 'a date with destiny', insofar as it took place on a Labour Day holiday, and Jim's thirty-ninth birthday, the Krickstein match was played on live television, and in front of '20,000 people making the noise of 60,000.' They witnessed four hours and forty-one minutes of seesawing drama—a match of amazing winners and diabolical errors, of nasty injuries and endless fist pumps. They witnessed a match in which Krickstein won the first and third sets, and Connors managed to snatch back the second and fourth.

When the twenty-four-year-old Krickstein took a 5–2 lead in the fifth set, it seemed like a safe bet that he'd take out the match. But Connors wasn't having any of that. With near-hysterical support from the crowd (at one point he stared directly into the TV camera, and yelled, 'This is what they paid for, this is what they want'), the bad-boy-come-good unleashed a series of extraordinary winners, and finally took out the extraordinary match.

Mind you, he wouldn't have won any prizes for good manners. The whole dramatic spectacle was capped off by Connors's ongoing chats with the chair umpire, which, it has to be said, weren't always polite. Some of his more pleasant remarks to that 'bum' (who was also a 'son of a bitch') included 'Get the fuck out of there' and 'Don't give me that crap.' Plus everybody's favourite: 'You're an abortion.'

All pretty vile, really. But what the hell, it was fun to watch.

Pete Sampras versus Jim Courier
Australian Open quarter final, 1995

Until 24 January 1995, the number of memorable games involving Pete Sampras could be counted on less than one hand. Once described as being 'as dumb as a box of hair'—a description that some may see as generous—Pistol Pete didn't seem to have too many thoughts when he was out on the court, and those that he had, he kept to himself.

That fateful 1995 Australian Open quarter final started out like any other Sampras match: a tidy, efficient performance of the very highest standard, but without any of the theatre that makes good tennis great. The only unusual thing was that Sampras wasn't winning. Two-time Australian Open champion Jim Courier had taken out the first two sets in two closely fought tie breaks, then the world number one had clawed back the third and the fourth. If the dour and unsmiling Sampras ever changed his facial expression during this period, it was so he could instead look unsmiling and dour.

It was in the fifth set that the facade finally cracked—and it was all thanks to an outspoken fan. 'Do it for your coach, Pete,' someone from the crowd yelled out, while Sampras was getting ready to serve.

And blow me down if Pete didn't burst into tears.

His coach, you see, was Tim Gullikson, a long-time friend and mentor. A long-time friend and mentor who had earlier that day been diagnosed with a brain tumour and flown back to hospital for urgent treatment.

On prime-time TV, and in a packed centre court, the planet's best and most private player just stood there with a shiny, wet face, eyes weeping, chest heaving, face crumpled with sorrow and pain. Every single emotion inside his head was on his face, on show to the world. 'C'mon, honey, get in there,' called his girlfriend from the front row. 'Are you all right, Pete? We can do this tomorrow,' called out Courier himself.

As it happened, he *was* alright. Sampras walked off the court, and splashed water on his face, and then came back and served a big ace. He kept crying throughout that entire final set … and he kept hitting aces and winners. The final score was 6–7 (7–4), 6–7 (7–3), 6–3, 6–4, 6–3.

'It would certainly be one of the few, if not the best, I've played as far as the intensity and quality of play,' Courier said later. 'The level of tennis was exceptional in that match and just high drama all the way through. And a really great sense of camaraderie after the match which Pete and I shared in the locker room having been through that together.'

'I think people understand that I'm normal, I have feelings like everyone else … I'm not a robot out there,' said Sampras a few days later, after beating Michael Chang in the semifinal. 'I'm as normal as the guy across the street, and I think that's what people have to realise, when they see tennis players, we're not above everyone, we do the same things everyone else does.'

Goran Ivanisevic versus Pat Rafter
Wimbledon final, 2001

If you were designing a machine to win Wimbledon, you would give it Goran Ivanisevic's serve. Responsible for over 10,000 career aces—a figure unsurpassed by any player in history—it was a high-bouncing, fast-swerving thunderbolt that routinely topped 120 miles per hour. Goran's service games could last less than two minutes. On a good day, they'd be done in one.

It was not altogether surprising, then, to see Goran reach three Wimbledon finals by the age of twenty-seven.

But it was also not that surprising when he lost every one. With his so-so forehand, slightly dodgy backhand, and a brittle temperament that tended to snap, Goran could spend more time on court cursing himself than actually concentrating on the game. By age twenty-nine, he was without a Grand Slam—or, indeed, a place in the top 100. With a shoulder injury that would soon require surgery (and very soon end his career), Goran was a has-been who never quite *had* been, a chronic underachiever with a still-cracking serve.

But Wimbledon is nothing if not nostalgic, and when the world number 125 asked for a wildcard, organisers duly complied. It turned out to be a good decision. Unless you were a star like Carlos Moyá, Andy Roddick, Tim Henman or Greg Rusedski. All of whom Goran managed to beat on his way to the final.

But it was that final against Australia's Pat Rafter that most people remember—a seesawing, bowel-clenching battle between two serve-volleyers who didn't really do rallies, just charged at the net. Adding to the atmosphere was probably the most noisy and un-Wimbledon-like crowd that the tournament had ever seen at the final. Because rain had washed out the traditional Sunday final—a staid affair packed with corporate boxes—many tickets had been made available to whoever happened to turn up on the day. Most of those people turned out to be expats—and to have come direct from the pub. With faces painted and clown hats on, the crowd clapped, cheered and chanted. And waved flags and sang songs and danced. 'I don't know if Wimbledon has seen anything like it,' Rafter commented afterwards. 'I don't know if they will again. It was electric.'

'So many Australian fans and Croatians, like a [soccer] match,' Ivanisevic said. 'The crowd was just too good.'

The *umpires*, on the other hand, left Goran less than impressed—not least when he was facing a break in the fourth. He served an ace ... which was called a fault ... and screamed 'Noooooooooooo!' at the top of his voice. Finally, slowly, he then got it together. Then served another ace and started to celebrate. Only to stop when it was called a double-fault. Game: Rafter. Tantrum: Ivanisevic. The big Croatian 'got a little crazy' after this, as he later admitted, hurling his racquet and kicking the net and having a somewhat audible 'chat' with the umpire.

But he eventually got back on track. In fact, he did better than that: he won the match 6–3, 3–6, 6–3, 2–6, 9–7. 'I don't care now if I ever win a match in my life again,' said the comeback kid, in a victory speech that was hard to hear over the roar of the crowd. 'Whatever I do in my life, wherever I go, I'm always going to be Wimbledon champion.'

He never won a tournament again.

John Isner versus Nicolas Mahut
Wimbledon first round, 2010

'This one's obviously going to stick with me probably the rest of my life, really,' said the big-serving American John Isner, after his famous game against Nicolas Mahut. 'But I hope it doesn't define my career. I think I have what it takes, you know, to do some really big things in this game. The four biggest tournaments of the year are the Grand Slams. I have probably a good seven, eight years left to try to make a good run at 'em. So hopefully this won't be the thing that I'm most remembered about.'

Sorry, John, but I suspect it will.

When the twenty-five-year-old American met the twenty-eight-year-old Frenchman in the first round of Wimbledon, not too many fans brought along a seatbelt so they could strap themselves in. Both players were, well, journeymen. Isner was a six-foot-nine-inch serving machine who had only turned pro after college. His best effort at a Grand Slam was to once make the third round. Mahut was a former child prodigy whose career had more or less peaked at eighteen. Ten years later, he had won zero titles and was ranked number 148 in the world.

So no-one was expecting a classic. But a classic was what everyone got. An absolute masterclass in the art of serving (perhaps helped by the fact that neither man was much good at returns), the match lasted an astonishing *eleven* hours, due to the fact that neither player could break the other one's serve in the fifth set. That makes it far and away the longest match in the history of tennis, and the source of all sorts of other records as well. The longest set (70–68!). The most games in a match (183). The most aces in a match (216!). The most aces by one player (Isner: 113). The most points scored by one player (Mahut: 502).

Isner won the point that counted, though—that being the last one of the match. After punching that down-the-line winner, he celebrated appropriately ... by collapsing in an exhausted heap on the grass. For his part, Mahut simply sat down. With a towel draped over his face. The final score was 6–4, 3–6, 6–7, 7–6, 70–68.

But when it came to sportsmanship, both players won. 'It's really painful,' Mahut told the crowd. 'We played the greatest match ever, in the greatest place to play tennis. I thought he would make a mistake. I waited for that moment, and it never came.'

'The guy's an absolute warrior,' added Isner. 'It stinks someone had to lose. To share this with him was an absolute honour. Maybe we'll meet again somewhere down the road and it won't be 70–68.'

As it happens, the visibly exhausted Isner went on to break another record just two days later, in the second round. Requiring continual treatment for neck and shoulder strains, not to mention a massive blister on his toe, he was thrashed by Thiemo de Bakker in less than seventy-five minutes . . . the, um, shortest Wimbledon match of all time.

A journalist asked Isner what he planned to do next and got a predictable answer. 'I'll watch sports, I'll take in the World Cup, I'll go fishing, I'll do whatever. Just anything away from the tennis court!'

-8-

THE GRAND TANTRUMS

As the parent of two young children, I like to talk a lot about the value of good manners. 'Temper tantrums don't impress anyone,' I tell Henry (aged five) and Eliza (aged four). 'Courtesy and respect are how you achieve things in life. The world belongs to those who say "please".'

Deep down, we all know that I'm lying. And just as Henry and Eliza are more likely to get ice-cream if they stomp, cry and whinge, tennis players know that they're more likely to get a win if they can let off a bit of steam.

And even if they lose, it's still fun to watch. Sophisticated tennis fans obviously deplore all those crass, loud vulgarians who swear at umpires and smash racquets. But that doesn't mean we don't like them as well.

Ilie Năstase
US Open third round, 1976

Before John McEnroe broke the record for fines and suspensions, it was held by one Ilie Năstase. And it has to be said that he held it with style. Able to insult umpires in six different languages, 'Nasty's' career achievements included mooning a referee, throwing a shoe at a line judge, and almost getting into fistfights with at least four players. Heckling his opponents was a Năstase speciality—he called Cliff Richey 'an animal', Arthur Ashe 'the black man'—but he was more than happy to heckle spectators as well. 'I think if somebody screams at me from the crowd, I should be able to scream at them too,' he liked to tell journalists … when he wasn't abusing them, too.

'He is a man with a very brittle psyche,' is how the tennis writer Bud Collins put it. 'What he does isn't calculated. I don't think he can control himself.'

Maybe, or maybe not. All we can say for certain when it comes to the Romanian wild child was that he did his best work at Flushing Meadows. Nasty's 1976 US Open match against Hans-Jürgen Pohmann was fairly incident-free during the first set, until a spectator yelled out something distracting which lost him a point. Năstase made his displeasure known by abusing said spectator. And a few other spectators. And the umpire. And a ball boy. And some courtside photographers. He also swung his racquet at the umpire, hit a couple of balls into the crowd, and 'flung obscene gestures in all directions'.

That, of course, left just Pohmann to deal with—the German had so far got off scot-free. All that changed in the third set, when Năstase's opponent was hit with bad cramps. He fell to the floor no less than three times, clutching his leg and writhing in pain. The umpire duly called for a doctor. And Năstase duly called the umpire a cheat. 'Is not football!' he screamed. 'No time out!'

When Năstase finally won the match (because Pohman could hardly move), he spat some orange juice at his beaten opponent and then called him a 'son of bitch'. He then followed those words up with a bit of a shove, and a 'Fuck you, Hitler' in case his feelings weren't clear.

'In all my years, I have never seen such deplorable behaviour,' said a pearl-wearing, very proper old lady, who somehow managed to make herself heard over the boos of the crowd.

Năstase's reply?

'Fuck you, bitch.'

THE GRAND TANTRUMS

Jimmy Connors
US Open final, 1977

Some people called Jimmy Connors the 'Brash Basher of Belleville'.

Other people called him a knob.

'The most foul-mouthed player in the history of professional tennis' and 'the least popular player of his era', Connors argued with simply *everybody*. Umpires and linespeople. Players and officials. Members of the players union and members of the crowd. He also liked to strut about court with a racquet handle between his legs ... and occasionally give it a tug.

'There were times on court when ... I felt I could easily strangle him,' John McEnroe once said of his crass compatriot. But Mac would have had to go to the back of a very long queue.

For all that he liked giving linespeople the finger, Jimbo's finest moment may have come during a tournament in Maryland, when he noticed a teenager in the crowd kissing a former *Playboy* Playmate of the Year ... who just happened to be Jimbo's wife. Flinging his racquet to one side, the Brash Basher leapt into the stands and did some brash bashing: yanking the boy's hair as hard as he could and delivering a punch to the chin.

But enough of that incident. This book is called *Grand Slams of Tennis*, not *Obscure Tournaments in What I Think Is An East-Coast American State But May In Fact Be A City or Province*. So let's look at Jim's work in the Slams. As far as pure, unadulterated poor sportsmanship goes, it is hard to go past his performance in the 1977 US Open semifinal, back when the tournament was played on clay. When his Italian opponent challenged a line call by pointing to a mark on the court, Connors ran to his side of the net and quickly erased it, before the chair umpire could come take a look.

But as a spectacle, it was Jimbo's next match—the final, against Guillermo Vilas—that lingers most in the mind. It takes a lot to make an American crowd root against an American, but Connors managed it just by being himself. Dozens of cheering fans ran onto the court when the Argentine baseliner finally took out the match, and paraded him around on their shoulders.

But Jimbo wasn't there to see it. Furious about the line call that went against him on match point, he'd stalked out of the stadium before the presentation ceremony had even begun.

John McEnroe
Australian Open fourth round, 1990

When the *Sun* newspaper described the teenage John McEnroe as 'the most vain, ill-tempered, petulant loudmouth that the game of tennis has ever known', quite a few people agreed.

But by the end of his career, things were very different. Now *everybody* agreed.

The brash, ugly face of tennis throughout the late seventies and early eighties, McEnroe has become synonymous with the catchphrase 'You cannot be serious!' But he was actually just as likely to call someone a 'jerk', a 'moron' or an 'incompetent fool' (though my personal favourite is 'fucking communist asshole'). One of his more eloquent outbursts at Wimbledon actually caused Prince Charles's then fiancé, Lady Diana, to leave the Royal Box because 'her ears were no longer virgin'.

But for all of his swearing and spitting and screaming and sooking, Superbrat was in many ways at his most obnoxious during those rare moments when he shut up. However badly he might have lost his temper, McEnroe always managed to find it when he had to—that is, when he was about to earn a fourth code violation, and thus be disqualified from the match. 'He'd never allow himself to be thrown out of a tournament,' says tennis official Randy Gregson. 'He was always like a little kid who'd tempt you and tempt you and tempt you but stop just short of making you take the final step.'

The one glorious exception to this rule happened in Melbourne, during a famous Australian Open match against

Mikael Pernfors. It was a not-untypical Mac effort, which saw him smash one racquet and throw another and yell at a baby who was crying in the crowd. He also earned a code violation for unsportsmanlike conduct after glaring at a lineswoman for what seemed like eternity, while bouncing a ball on his racquet rather threateningly.

But all that was just another day at the office: all a bit same old, same old, really. What made this fourth-round match so famous was the fact that the tantrum rules had recently changed. Now players were only permitted to have *three* code violations before being disqualified. And Big Mac wasn't aware.

So when he earned a second code violation (for more racquet-throwing) in the fourth set, Superbrat naturally told the tournament official to 'go fuck [his] mother'. The worst that could happen, he figured, was that he'd earn a third violation and thus be penalised a game.

He figured wrong. Mac instead became the first player in the Australian Open's eighty-five-year history to be kicked out of the tournament for misconduct.

'I don't have anybody to blame but myself,' he said later, to general agreement all round. 'I probably wouldn't have said what I said to the guy if I had known I was one step from being defaulted. They've written the rules for me. It was not like they wrote the rules for anybody else. It was bound to happen. I can't say I'm totally surprised by what they did.'

And I can't say I'm totally sorry.

Tim Henman
Wimbledon second round, 1995

Tim Henman was never a bad boy. If he had a fault, it was being too good. The floppy-haired son of an Oxfordshire solicitor, Henman was like something straight out of a Hugh Grant movie: trim, prim and privately educated, well-spoken and slightly dull.

He was a champion that England's middle classes could take to their heart, and that people from Liverpool wanted to kick in the balls.

Mind you, Tim was capable of violence himself at times. Well ... at *one* time ... more or less by accident. It is a strange but true fact that the only player to ever be kicked out of Wimbledon was Mr Head Prefect himself.

The incident happened during a doubles match way back in 1995, at the then nineteen-year-old's second Wimbledon. There was no Henman Hill to cheer him on in those days: just Dad (navy blazer, V-neck sweater) and Mum (bouffy hair and pearls).

They saw their boy mis-hit a volley—and react by giving the ball a bit of a whack. Straight into the head of a sixteen-year-old ball girl, who, unbeknown to Tim, was crouched just a few feet away. She fell to the ground, crying. Then ran back to her position, crying still. All in all, it wasn't great publicity (or even that funny, after the first few minutes).

In response to urging from Jeff Tarango and Henrik Holm, the doubles team on the other side of the net, the umpire eventually defaulted Tim and his partner Jeremy Bates 'on the basis of unsportsmanlike conduct'. The crowd booed heartily ... but you could almost hear the tabloid editors let out a cheer.

'It's a complete accident, but I'm responsible for my actions,' said Tim at a packed press conference the next day, after some headlines that probably still give him nightmares. The twenty-year-old presented the ball girl with a massive bouquet of flowers—and an apologetic kiss, at the prompting of photographers.

'Two things came out of that,' Henman reflected years later.

That was my first real taste of the media and I got absolutely crucified. I got absolutely slaughtered for 48 hours or something. It was a joke, there were these headlines saying, 'He hit it so hard it could have killed her'. I was like, 'Come on, please!' It was a complete accident. It never happened before and it has never happened since, in any tournament. I think it is safe to say it was pretty unlucky. And the fact that we were two sets to one up. We were winning, it wasn't like we were losing and I was pissed off or anything.

The other thing that came out of that, all the coverage and notoriety that came out of that, being the first person to be disqualified from Wimbledon, I kind of said to myself, 'Shit, I'm going to have to produce some results, because this is not how I want to be remembered.'

But now it is interesting, when I speak to people—not that I bring it up that often—if you asked them who was the first person to be disqualified from Wimbledon, I don't think too many of them would know that it was me.

Jeff Tarango
Wimbledon third round, 1995

There was only one difference between Jeff Tarango and John McEnroe. Jeff Tarango wasn't very good at tennis.

This was probably the main reason why Jeff found himself losing to Germany's world number 115, Alexander Mronz, during their Wimbledon match in 1996, but the balding Californian preferred to blame the linesmen. And when one of those linesmen called one of his serves a 'fault', when any honest man would have clearly thought 'ace', this high-level conspiracy against him just became too much for a man to bear.

The infuriated Tarango argued and argued with umpire Bruno Rebeuh, to the point where the crowd began to whistle and boo. This, you may not be surprised to learn, had the effect of infuriating him even more. 'Shut up,' he yelled at the top of his voice.

'Code violation, audible obscenity, Mr Tarango,' was Mr Rebeuh's prompt reply.

Outrageous, yes? Appalled by this latest injustice, Tarango

stormed over to his chair and sat down in a huff. 'No, no, no, I'm not playing anymore,' he told umpire Rebeuh, and demanded that he fetch the tournament supervisor. The supervisor was fetched, more words were exchanged, and then these words were uttered for all to hear. 'You are the most corrupt official in the game!' screamed Tarango.

Which resulted in another code violation for verbal abuse.

Which resulted in the American picking up his bags and storming off the court.

But that's not all, folks. If behind every great man there's a great woman, it seems that behind every mad man there's a crazy one. Having watched the drama unfold from the player's box, Jeff's wife decided to get in on the act. She waylaid umpire Rebeuh on his way to the dressing room and proceeded to slap him, twice, on the face.

'I don't think it's bad,' said Benedicte Tarango at a well-attended press conference later that day. 'I think it's good. This guy deserves a lesson at some point. He can do whatever he wants because he's on the chair. It's not fair. He's a bad person. If Jeff slaps him, he's out of the tennis tour, so I do it.'

By now Jeff had had time to calm down a little bit. But you'll be glad to know that he hadn't. 'I applaud you doing that,' said husband to wife, before launching into a complicated conspiracy theory to the effect that Rebeuh was in fact Satan.

'I don't feel that I should be pushed around for my whole life and let people take advantage of me. I just felt that I was backed into a corner and that I had no recourse for defending myself.'

Damn right, Jeff. Someone give that man a medal.

Martina Hingis
French Open final, 1999

Tennis players can be quite forgiving of 'bad etiquette'. When Marcos Baghdatis systematically smashed four racquets at the

2012 Australian Open, for example, the general reaction among his colleagues was something in between admiration and respect. 'That's impressive. Wow,' said Serena Williams, while Novak Djokovic found it 'great to watch'.

Some things, however, are simply *not done* in tennis, and one of them is crossing the net. If you are going to invade your opponent's side of the court, you may as well go the whole hog and sleep with their mother. And then put the footage on YouTube and release a statement criticising her technique. *It is just not done.*

Except, of course, when it *is*. In 1999, Martina Hingis was an Australian Open, US Open and Wimbledon champion ... and she was still only just eighteen. 'Steffi has had some results in the past, but it's a faster, more athletic game now than when she played. She is old now. Her time has passed,' said the Swiss Miss of the thirty-year-old Steffi Graf, whose number-one spot she now owned. Hingis was a girl with the world at her feet and, as such, she didn't take disappointment well.

But disappointment lay in store.

It took the form of having a forehand called 'out' at that year's French Open final against none other than Steffi Graf. No biggie, you would think, as Hingis was in front by a set and a break, but *you*, reader, would not be Martina. An enraged Hingis crossed the net to show the line judge where she thought the ball had landed. And, in doing so, she enraged the crowd.

From that point forth, they booed when she served, and they booed when she received. They jeered at her errors and they hissed at her winners. You don't want to mess with the French, my friends. (Unless we're talking about war. In that case, you're fine.)

The cumulative result of this treatment was what can only be described as a mental collapse: from 6–4, 2–0 up, Hingis proceeded to lose the second set, and leave the court for a fifteen-minute 'toilet break' in the third. When she reappeared, it was in a brand-new outfit—but it was the same story when play resumed. Hingis's meltdown ended with her serving underarm, and collapsing into tears when Graf took out the match. She stormed off the court before the awards presentation, and had to be dragged back on by her mum.

Lleyton Hewitt
US Open second round, 2001

Okay, Lleyton's mellowed a lot in recent years, and become an elder statesman of the game.

But I think we're all allowed to remember the good times. These obviously include that press conference where he slammed 'the stupidity of the Australian public', and that French Open match where he called the chair umpire a 'spastic'.

'It's the only way I know to play sport,' says the fist-pumping Aussie, a man who listens to 'Eye of the Tiger' from *Rocky III* before every match, and likes to fire himself up by shouting 'C'mon Rock!' 'I need to be in that mood to play my best tennis ... I like to show emotion and not everyone likes it.'

'We all know how Lleyton is,' Argentina's Guillermo Coria once commented, in a tone that did not imply total approval. 'He can be the best player in the world, win every tournament, but I would not want to be like him.' Hewitt's habit of celebrating every point—even if he's won it thanks to an opponent's mistake—for many years made him heartily disliked 'by every other player on the international circuit'.

He may also not have a fan in a certain linesman. Lleyton's worst-ever headlines undoubtedly occurred during the 2001 US Open, after a five-set victory over American James Blake. Or, more to the point, the African American James Blake.

The linesman, as it happens, was also black, and Hewitt didn't much like it when he called him out for two foot faults. 'Look at him,' Hewitt said to umpire Andres Egli, pointing to the linesman. 'And look at him,' pointing at Blake. 'You tell me what the similarity is. You put him off the court. Get him off the court.'

'It was a terrible act,' says tennis writer Bud Collins. 'Everybody knew what he meant.'

'The thing is, he's a big foot faulter,' added his colleague Mary Carillo. 'So the idea that all of a sudden, in the heat of a match, he's getting called for it out of racial bias was ridiculous.'

Hewitt's press conference could have been a good time to say sorry, but Rock instead chose to slug it out. 'It was a conversation between me and the umpire,' he maintained defiantly. 'I come from a multi-cultured country. I'm not racial in any way. People can have their own opinions, there was nothing racial said out there. You can all think what you want.'

Okay, Lleyton. We will.

Greg Rusedski
Wimbledon second round, 2003

'I lost it a little bit,' said Greg Rusedski, in what you might call a little bit of an understatement. 'I didn't handle it the best I could and I regret it. For people who were offended, I apologise.'

The usually mild-mannered Canadian (who managed to annoy all of Canada by becoming a British citizen) was here talking about an incident during his Wimbledon match against Andy Roddick, in which he aired a few thoughts a few feet from a TV camera.

Rusedski's first thought was that some people in the crowd shouldn't have yelled 'out' during a crucial rally—and especially not when the ball was in. His second thought was that the umpire should order a replay of the point. And his third thought was that the umpire's refusal to do so was fairly unreasonable.

Intelligent observers of the live TV coverage could gauge all this by the way he screamed, 'I can't do anything if the crowd fucking calls it. Absolutely fucking ridiculous. At least replay the point.'

And even *un*intelligent observers could have picked up on his general mood after he added, 'Fucking ridiculous, fucking ridiculous, frigging ridiculous. Some wanker in the crowd changes the whole match and you allow it to happen. Well done, well done, well done. Absolutely shit.'

Needless to say, it was excellent television—though it didn't do much for the match. Rusedski barely won another point after the rant, losing his serve for the first and second time in the match, and then losing the whole match itself. He stormed off the court with steam still coming out of his ears, presumably muttering something along the lines of 'fucking ridiculous'.

The BBC later had to apologise for any offence caused by its coverage—'In a live broadcast there is always a danger,' said a spokesman—and then it was Rusedski's turn. 'I'm a professional and I should not have let it happen,' he said in a press conference. 'Sometimes your emotions just take control.'

Well, yes. Quite.

Serena Williams
US Open final, 2011

'You're a hater and you're just unattractive inside.'

No, that was not Serena Williams talking about herself. That was Serena talking to an umpire during the 2011 US Open final, after she got a code violation that she didn't much like.

But that wasn't the end of their little chat—a chat which began when Serena yelled out 'come on' after hitting what she thought would be a winner against Samantha Stosur, even though the ball was still technically in play. Under Grand Slam rules, an 'intentional shout' mid-rally leads to a code violation. But under Serena rules, that's simply not on.

'If you ever see me walking down the hall, look the other way, because you're out of control. You're out of control. You're totally out of control,' she yelled at the umpire, showing herself to be a master of repetition, the rhetorical device so beloved by the Greeks.

'Who would do such a thing?' she added. 'And I never complain. Wow. What a loser … We're in America last I checked. Can I get a water, or am I gonna get violated for a water? Really, don't even look at me! I promise you, don't look at me. Don't look my way.'

In insisting that she never complains, Serena may have been using another ancient rhetorical device called 'lying'. The brash American has received a record number of fines for behaviour violations over the years. However good she may be at tennis, it's at the sport of complaining that she really excels.

Take her equally famous outburst at the 2009 US Open, when she was down match point to Kim Clijsters … and received a line call that she didn't quite like. 'I swear to God, I'm fucking going to take this fucking ball and shove it down your fucking throat,' she told the rather petite, middle-aged Asian lineswoman, pointing a meaty finger right at her face. 'You hear that? I swear to God.'

A regrettable incident, all in all, but you'll be glad to hear that it taught her a lesson. 'I got really popular,' Serena later reflected. 'A lot of people were telling me they thought I was super cool, that they never saw me so intense, so, yeah, it was awesome.'

- 9 -
LIFE OFF THE COURT

Unless you're someone like Pete Sampras, there's a lot more to life than hitting a ball. Here's what some players do with theirs.

Sleeping with each other

Opinion is divided about whether you should have sex before sport (though most of us agree that it's fun). Boris Becker is certainly in the 'yes' camp. As a nineteen-year-old, he defied his coach's instructions to stay away from his partner during Wimbledon—and was knocked out in the second round.

But tennis players aren't actually *able* to stay away from their partners, even those who (like so many of us) would actually quite like to. This is because their partners are often players as well. 'It's kind of an incestuous world,' said sports psychologist John Mayer of the pro tennis circuit—a world of 'very adolescent' and short-lived relationships in which the men tend to behave like 'Neanderthals' and the women like 'giggly Jonas Brothers fans'.

If you want proof, then look at Radek Štěpánek. He's been engaged to Martina Hingis during his decade on the circuit and dated Nicole Vaidišová and Petra Kvitová as well. The Czech says that his fatal attractiveness comes down to 'who I am as a person'. And, having seen his face, I suspect that he's right.

Spain's Fernando Vedasco is another lady-killer, having dated Ana Ivanovic and Gisela Dulko; while Dominika Cibulková has been doing her bit for the womenfolk, dating Jürgen Melzer and Gaël Monfils. Other present-day tennis couples include

Maria Sharapova and Grigor Dimitrov, Márta Domachowska and Jerzy Janowicz, and Sloane Stephens and Jack Sock.

You would think that the name 'Jack Sock' be would a good reason to break up with someone. So is discovering them in bed with a TV presenter. This, alas, was the experience of Carlos Moyá's girlfriend Flavia Pennetta—and she did not take the discovery well. 'People felt sorry for me and I could not even defend myself,' Pennetta wrote of her turbulent break-up with Moyá, which saw her lose a great deal of weight. 'It was as if I had lost my taste for things. I was trying to be numb towards life, not to feel pain. I did not even feel physical pain. A silly example: even when I was waxing, I did not even feel anything.'

Martina Hingis's relationships with Julián Alonso, Ivo Heuberger, Magnus Norman and Radek Štěpánek may have also involved some questionable bedroom antics, if her estranged husband is to be believed. 'Martina has a very personal conception of morality,' says the former Mr Hingis, Thibault Hutin, who said he'd twice caught the Swiss Miss with another man. 'She has always been like that; I think she has always been unfaithful to her boyfriends.'

And perhaps violent, too? Hutin also maintains that Hingis and her mother physically assaulted him on one occasion, and then threatened to 'set the Russians on him' after he fled. 'I have bruises and scratches on the neck, head and right forearm,' he told the Swiss newspaper *Blick*. 'I'm really scared and asking myself, what comes next—a bullet?'

This may be a question for Jimmy Connors to ask himself—Chris Evert certainly won't be sending him a Christmas card. The loved-up American stars were all set to marry back in 1974, only to very abruptly call off the wedding. For some forty years, no-one quite knew why. And then Connors decided to tell us. 'An issue had arisen as a result of youthful passion, and a decision had to be made as a couple,' he wrote in his recent autobiography. 'Chrissie called to say she was taking care of the "issue". I was happy to let nature take its course. It was a horrible feeling, but I knew it was over. Getting married wasn't going to be good for us.'

Classy guy.

Sleeping with celebrities

Philosophers have always argued about the meaning of life. Is it about happiness? Is it about morality? Is it about achieving some sort of spiritual awareness? Or serving others? Or pleasing some god?

Let's end the discussion right here and now. Life is clearly about sleeping with celebrities. And this is something that tennis players do well.

If you have any doubts, just ask Chris Evert. She's has been married to three well-known sportsmen: golfer Greg Norman, skier Andy Mill and fellow tennis star John Lloyd—and engaged to a fourth, in Jimmy Connors. She's also clocked up relationships with a rock star (Adam Faith) and a Hollywood star (Burt Reynolds), and found time to see a US president's son (Jack Ford). 'I haven't been alone since I was 21,' says the now-alone Evert, who has started seeing a therapist in recent years. 'I've had boyfriends and husbands—if I was an addict in anything, I was a relationship addict. It wasn't a need for love, because I had that. What I needed was approval, affirmation. I think that's probably why I always needed to be in a relationship. A lot of it was my neediness.'

Rory McIlroy, on the other hand, does *not* need to be in a relationship. Or, at least, not one with Caroline Wozniacki. The British golfer and the Danish tennis star were all set to marry in late 2014, until he broke off the engagement in a three-minute phone call. 'The problem is mine,' Rory later said to the media. 'The wedding invitations issued at the weekend made me realise that I wasn't ready for all that marriage entails. I wish Caroline all the happiness she deserves and thank her for the great times we've had.'

Great.

Serbian star Ana Ivanovic also had some great times with a golfer, Australia's Adam Scott, but the glamour couple split in 2012. 'They are both constantly travelling,' an 'insider' told the women's magazines. 'It was just a matter of geography in the end, really.'

Lifelong bachelor Cliff Richard may have other issues that prevent him from getting married—but apparently, he once came close. The Peter Pan of Pop says he 'seriously contemplated asking [1976 French Open winner] Sue Barker to marry me, but in the end I realised that I didn't love her quite enough to commit the rest of my life to her.'

Is that what's stopping Anna Kournikova from getting hitched? We need an insider to say what's going on there. The former Russian star has been dating Spanish superhunk Enrique Iglesias for fourteen years without going anywhere near an aisle.

Perhaps they both need to change their agents? Andy Roddick would still be a bachelor, after all, if he hadn't had good help on hand. When the US Open winner saw busty model and actress Brooklyn Decker on the cover of *Sports Illustrated*, he got *his* agent to call *her* agent to see if she'd like to go on a date.

Hopefully, there were no agents involved in Andre Agassi's marriage to Steffi Graf—but he certainly needed a lawyer when he divorced Brooke Shields. The couple were together for a famously troubled two years. And then, very abruptly, they weren't. 'I had a thought that no man should have on his wedding day,' Agassi later wrote of his walk down the aisle. 'I wished that I had a decoy groom to take my place.'

Sleeping with anything that moves

'I think I've slept with about 2500 women,' says the 1970s star Ilie Năstase of his evidently action-packed youth. 'Sex in those days was like taking a daily shower—you take one, it feels nice, then you forget it ... I had a great time, but I cannot remember much. If I remembered every girl then I'd be a genius. I know I had a lot of girls, but I was not the only one, everyone did the same.'

Well, 'everyone' is probably an exaggeration—but the 1970s does seem to have had groupies. Just ask Jimmy Connors, who was 'unfaithful' to Chris Evert. And a Miss World. And a *Playboy* model.

Or ask his compatriots Arthur Ashe and Roscoe Tanner—two men who were much more than doubles partners. They were also a great team *off* the court, cruising singles bars and Playboy Clubs almost every night in search of a girl with a pulse. 'I witnessed beautiful women gravitating toward [Ashe] like James Bond, and all I had to do was pick up the leftovers,' wrote Tanner, a man who was described by one of his many wives as having a sex addiction after he accidentally impregnated a prostitute.

Boris Becker, of course, knows all about accidental offspring. The German famously met a model in a London restaurant the day he retired from tennis—and then got to know her very well in a nearby broom cupboard. 'She looked directly at me, the look of the hunter that said, "I want you",' he later wrote of the encounter ... which, um, happened while his pregnant wife was in hospital.

'Then there she was again, walking twice past the bar. And again this look. A little while later she left her table for the toilet. I followed behind. Five minutes small talk and then straight away into the nearest possible place and down to business. Afterwards she went off, I had another beer, paid and went back to my hotel. As there wasn't any news from the hospital I went to bed around 2 am.'

Sadly for the tabloid newspapers, today's players go to bed a lot earlier than that. The closest we've come to 'SCANDAL!' in recent years are YouTube videos of Bernard Tomic enjoying a lap dance, and fighting a semi-nude dude in a hot tub. Though to be fair, Ernests Gulbis also did his bit by spending a night in a Swedish jail for soliciting a prostitute.

And while the French Open winner Francesca Schiavone hasn't given us any great headlines, she does at least give a good quote. 'For a woman, sex before a match is not only allowed, it is fantastic,' she maintained in an interview with England's *Metro* website. 'It raises your hormone levels and brings advantages to all of your points. In recent years I have grown, and my feminine side is a lot more visible. But it is a gift reserved for just a few.'

Sorry about that, Roscoe.

Criticising each other's personalities

If you don't have anything nice to say, say something nasty instead. That seemed to be the attitude of Zambian tennis player Lighton Ndefwayl after he lost a match to one of his compatriots. 'Musumba Bwayla is a stupid man and a hopeless player, he has a huge nose and is cross-eyed, and girls hate him,' said Ndefwayl at a memorable press conference. 'He beats me because my jockstrap was too tight and because when he serves, he farts, and that made me lose my concentration, for which I am famous throughout Zambia.'

John McEnroe would never have made that kind of excuse after losing to Brad Gilbert. But that's mainly because he would never have lost to Brad Gilbert. 'You don't deserve to be on the same court with me,' Superbrat famously told that somewhat mediocre player, during a match at Madison Square Garden. 'You're the worst, the fucking worst.'

Ivan Lendl, of course, was far from the fucking worst—but Mac didn't have much praise for him either. 'I've got more talent in my pinkie than Lendl has in his whole body,' the American once said of his Czech rival, who actually beat him more often than not. 'The guy hasn't been good for tennis. He's been so selfish. And he's certainly not the kind of guy who brings out the best in others. He's hurt the popularity of the game so much. Do you like a robot being the world number one?'

All in all, it's not hard to see why Jimmy Connors called McEnroe 'fuck face'. Though Arthur Ashe would have said that another reason was that Connors himself is 'an asshole'. 'I swear, every time I passed Connors in the locker room, it took all my willpower not to punch him in the mouth.'

Austria's Thomas Muster had similar issues with one of his countrymen, the little-known but apparently annoying Horst Skoff. 'I'd like one day to find myself within four walls alone with Horst and finally have a chance to hit him with a lot of punches until I knock him down,' Muster once told a journalist.

Left alone with Lleyton Hewitt, Guillermo Coria might have gone even further. 'You really feel like killing him,' he said after a Davis Cup tie between Argentina and Australia that must have had some tense moments. 'As a person, I would rather not win a single tournament in my life than be like him.'

Coria's teammate David Nalbandian was also happy to share some thoughts about Hewitt — 'nobody [on tour] is a friend of him' — but most of *his* dislike seems to be reserved for Tim Henman. 'All this selling himself as a gentleman is not true,' was the Argentine's crisp character summary of the English star. 'He is the worst rubbish there is.'

Saying such things to a journalist is generally a bad idea, as Ivan Ljubičić well knows. The former Croatian star neatly avoided an invitation to criticise Andy Roddick at a US Open press conference — and then thought 'What the hell' and gave it a go. 'I'm sorry if he's expecting everybody's going to like him. He thinks he's the best, the greatest, the most beautiful. But that's not the case … I mean, generally, I don't like him. I mean, not me, nobody in the locker room likes his acting on the court.'

And nobody much liked Pat Cash either, if Boris Becker is to be believed. 'Cash is not one of my favourite people,' said

Germany's favourite son, after beating the Aussie at Wimbledon in the late 1980s. 'He's one of the most aggressive, obnoxious players. I don't talk to him very often and I'm not the only one.'

Some female players probably belong in that group. Cash was once asked to give his opinion of the women's game—and happily complied in ten short words. 'Two sets of rubbish that lasts only half an hour.'

It was not, all things considered, a comment that went down well—but Cash had a firm supporter in Richard Krajicek. 'Eighty per cent of the top 100 women are fat pigs who don't deserve equal pay,' was the 1996 Wimbledon champion's contribution to the equal pay debate, though to his credit, he later apologised.

'What I meant to say was that *75 per cent* are fat pigs.'

Criticising each other's appearance

The 1994 Junior US Open featured a meeting between two future stars. Well, okay: one future star and one player who would eventually earn over $50 million in endorsements ... without ever actually winning a thing. But if Martina Hingis provided a sign of things to come, by embarrassing Anna Kournikova 6–0, 6–0, so did the beautiful Russian at the end of the match. 'You won,' Kournikova said when she went to shake hands, 'but I'm prettier and more marketable than you.'

It was a bad beginning to a relationship that then proceeded to get steadily worse. Newspaper reports even had the pair hurling trophies at each other during a locker-room catfight, along with a crystal vase which smashed on the floor. But don't go calling it a 'rivalry'. 'What rivalry?' Hingis said, after a reporter did just that. 'I always win.'

But winning isn't everything, if the French player Nathalie Tauziat is to be believed. In *The Underside of Women's Tennis*, she claimed that tournament organisers often give extra appearance money to the most marketable players—which is a very different category to the best. 'Aesthetics and charisma are winning out over sporting performance.'

And bitchiness has a role to play too. '[It's all about] who's the prettiest, who's the most popular, who's the most fashionable, who's getting the most coverage?' says Serbian star Ana Ivanovic of the WTA Tour. 'In the men's game, they're all friends. But we're not friends. You can be on the tour for ten years and still not be friends. It's sad.'

While Hingis was far from a people person (just ask her former doubles partner, who she ditched for being 'old and slow', or Amélie Mauresmo, who she called 'half a man'), she considers herself a lot nicer than today's version of Kournikova—the equally Russian, equally blonde and even-more-lavishly-sponsored Maria Sharapova, whom Hingis calls 'as mean as a snake'.

Sharapova herself rejects the comparison, but perhaps not in a way that inspires confidence. 'I'm not the next Kournikova,' she once told a journalist. 'I want to win matches.'

'It seems like everywhere you go, you're asked about Sharapova. All you read is about how elegant and graceful she is and how great her Wimbledon victory was for Russia. Quite frankly, I've had enough of that,' grumbles Svetlana Kuznetsova. 'If someone wants to make a fashion statement, they should go on stage and not on a tennis court.'

Though not all of her fashion statements are good ones, if Alla Kudryavtseva is to be believed. She once credited a win over Sharapova to the fact that Maria was wearing a faux tuxedo top. 'It was very pleasant to beat Maria. Why? I don't like her outfit. She's brave enough to experiment and I give her credit for that, but the outfit was a little bit too much of everything. It was one of the motivations to beat her.'

Part-time fashion student Venus Williams is always happy to offer fashion advice, whether or not it's required. 'That style was out last year,' she once said after beating a player in a one-sleeved shirt. 'It was something that was popular from the designers right down to the popular price level.'

An *affordable outfit*? Heaven forbid!

Dabbling in drugs

Not long after winning Wimbledon at the age of sixteen, Martina Hingis provided a few insights into life at the top. 'Once you start having a nice lifestyle from tennis, there are a lot of temptations,' the Swiss Miss confided. 'Once you make it on tour, you're going to beautiful places and staying in five-star hotels … and there are a lot of distractions all around you. So you have to watch out to make sure you don't become too comfortable … When you get older you know what it takes to stay disciplined.'

She quit tennis ten years later … after testing positive for cocaine.

Mind you, Martina's far from the only star to have had the big C in her system. The first players to be found guilty of having too good a time were Mats Wilander and Karel Nováček. Both men received three-month bans after failing a blood test during the 1995 French Open. 'It was the worst moment in my life,' says Nováček, who to this day denies any wrongdoing. 'I have tried to live the right way and to be a good son to my father. This is very sad for my parents.'

If Richard Gasquet was a married man in March 2009, his wife would have been very sad too. Fortunately, the French star was single when he attended a dance festival in Miami, and locked lips with a woman named Pamela. Or, more to the point, with a cokehead named Pamela. While Gasquet shortly afterwards tested positive for cocaine, he was cleared after authorities accepted that the substance had only made its way into his system because traces of it had been in Pam's mouth. 'We have found the player to be a person who is shy and reserved, honest and truthful and a man of integrity and good character,' the tribunal said in its ruling. 'He is neither a cheat nor a user of drugs for recreational purposes.'

Andre Agassi, on the other hand, *was* a user of drugs for recreational purposes—though he also found it a great help when cleaning his house. 'There is a moment of regret, followed by vast sadness,' he later wrote of his first experience with crystal meth. 'Then comes a tidal wave of euphoria that sweeps away every negative thought in my head. I've never felt so alive, so hopeful—and I've never felt such energy. I'm seized by a desperate desire to clean. I go tearing around my house, cleaning it from top to bottom. I dust the furniture. I scour the tub. I make the beds.'

Agassi had 'Slim' to thank for his sparkling clean house. The eight-time Grand Slam champion used meth for 'a year or so' after he came across his assistant having a snort—and Slim was also of great assistance when Agassi finally failed a drug test. 'I say Slim, whom I've since fired, is a known drug user, and that he often spikes his sodas with meth—which is true. Then I come to the central lie of the letter. I say that recently I drank accidentally from one of Slim's spiked sodas, unwittingly ingesting his drugs. I ask for understanding and leniency and hastily sign it: Sincerely. I feel ashamed, of course. I promise myself that this lie is the end of it.'

Miraculously, the tennis authorities believed him, and let the wayward star off the hook. But an even bigger miracle was that that really *was* the end of it. The depressed star managed to turn his life around and return to number one in the rankings after sinking as low as 141.

Agassi is far from the only star to use drugs to ward off anxiety. (And thus feel a little bit more anxiety. And therefore use more drugs to help ward it off.) Boris Becker spent years abusing alcohol and prescription medication 'in a desperate search for sleep'. 'I was sick,' says the former superstar, who won six Grand Slams but spent most of his career feeling 'melancholy'.

'In the early part of 1987 I couldn't take the pressure any more ... For the sleeplessness there was Planum, for the pain, [there were] a couple of other pills. Against the loneliness I felt with women, whisky. I had to occasionally reduce my tournament appearances to recover … from the effects of the pills. No one knew about all the chemicals affecting me.'

Plenty of people knew about all the chemicals affecting Jennifer Capriati, however. When the teenage star was arrested for marijuana possession in 1994, the papers let us know pretty quickly. 'I struggle with trying to like and love myself on a daily basis,' says the former child prodigy—who, like most child prodigies, had a God-awful childhood. 'I was at the height of my game … I was on top of the world, but something was still missing inside.'

'Smoking marijuana was commonplace among tennis players,' says Pat Cash, another player who coped with the demands of the tour by occasionally lighting up and having a toot. 'When I played my first time at Wimbledon, I'd keep a joint under my pillow and have a smoke every night. It calmed me down. The problem is that you think: "Drugs are supposed to be bad, but that smoke didn't ruin my game." So you take more. Then you take cocaine and the next drug and the next drug.'

And for those drugs, Cash turned to Vitas Gerulaitis—a top-ten player in the 1970s, when he wasn't busy carving up the dance floor. 'To me then, Vitas was quite simply The Man,' says Cash of the Ferrari-driving, model-shagging playboy, who would have won many more Slams than one Australian Open if he'd ever managed to wake up before midday. 'He lived to enjoy himself and was heavily into cocaine. His playing days were behind him but he was still very much part of the scene.'

He was also part of a federal grand jury investigation into drug dealing. 'Even when we were in junior, there were many rumours,' says his contemporary John McEnroe of 'Broadway Vitas', who often partied alongside Björn Borg at Studio 54. When McEnroe had his first night out on the town with the two men, he 'marked the occasion by indulging in something I'd never tried before (never mind what)—and the next thing I knew Vitas and Björn were carrying me back into the hotel. I felt sick but wonderful: I had passed the initiation.'

But enough of all this smut. In all fairness, it behoves this book to note that not all players just use drugs for fun. Take American Robert Kendrick, who tested positive for nandrolone, a performance-enhancing stimulant. As he later explained to the International Tennis Federation, he only took it for jet lag.

And who could doubt Mariano Hood's explanation for taking finasteride, a prohibited substance often used as a masking agent. He only took it to treat hair loss, as the tribunal heard.

Designing threads

Looks aren't everything—but, for Roger Federer, they still matter a lot. Already the most stylish *player* on the tour, the Swiss star is close chums with *Vogue*'s Anna Wintour, and clearly aspires to be the most stylish dresser. 'I started off wearing a lot of Prada and Dolce & Gabbana and Louis Vuitton [but] as you go along you try out lots of different designers,' says the budding fashionista. 'The most important thing is to feel comfortable in what you're wearing.'

Ok. Though is 'important' really the right word?

Yes.

'I try to look good on the tennis court too,' says Roger, who spends a great deal of time designing his playing clothes. 'I have a great relationship with Nike and together we try to create something that is cool and hip and new, that hasn't been done before. Hopefully people will look back and say "Roger helped the game of tennis in the way he looked on the court".'

Hopefully … Though for this to happen, humankind will need to enter an era in which wearing personalised monograms is socially acceptable. Federer's habit of putting his 'RF' logo everywhere—on his shoes, on his belt, on his racquet, embroidered in gold on a cashmere cardigan—has the tennis world divided. Some people find it a bit tacky. Other people say that it's vulgar.

But in Roger's defence, he's far from the first tennis player to boast a personalised monogram. Just consider the case of René Lacoste. That little crocodile that you see on Lacoste polo shirts is actually a reference to René himself: the man who founded the company was a French tennis player nicknamed 'the Crocodile'. The story goes that he once made a bet with his Davis Cup coach that he would win a particular match. The stakes were an alligator-skin suitcase that he'd seen in a store—and after he won it, teammates called him the Crocodile.

Equally famous in the fashion world is the last Englishman to win Wimbledon, Fred Perry. His rather dapper namesake label is, I'm told, considered 'the most British of brands'. Unlike Lacoste, however, who actually designed his own shirts, Fred just hopped on board the money train, after being approached by a businessman friend.

Björn Borg had a similar story. Though in his case, the train derailed. The Swede's Björn Borg fashion label sold underwear, clothing, footwear, bags, eyewear and fragrances. Or, at least, it did until it went bankrupt. A few years ago, however, Borg returned to the fashion industry, and is apparently enjoying quite a bit of success.

Can the word 'success' be used to describe Lleyton Hewitt's fashion label? Even if it makes billions, the answer is no. In December 2010, he teamed up with Inferno Sports to launch a brand of products called the C'MON range ... All feature a little picture of his famous fist pump and the slogan, 'Success and nothing less'.

Yawks ... But at least Inferno managed to avoid using the phase 'complex simplicity'. If it did, Serena Williams might sue. The American superstar is another tennis player who fancies herself as a fashion designer, recently launching (and then, um, relaunching) a label called Aneres. 'Aneres is for the independent

woman who works, enjoys life and is at the prime of her life,'
Williams says.

'I'm an unbelievable designer. I don't know how I know and
just do these things. I just start sketching and then I just know the
colours and I always know the forecast. I know green and purple
are going to be hot. I was born to be a designer. I worked hard to
be a tennis player, I don't work hard to be a designer.'

Losing money

'Money came in left, right and centre', says former Aussie ace
Mark Philippoussis of his time at the top of the tennis tree.
'I thought that's how it was for everyone and that's how it would
always be.'

It wasn't.

Less than a decade into retirement, the jet-setting, Paris
Hilton–shagging Australian no longer owns his yellow Ferrari.
Or, indeed, his black Lamborghini. Or his series of mansions all
over the globe. What he *does* own is a big, fat bankruptcy notice,
after defaulting on the mortgage on his Melbourne home.

'If I only knew a tenth of what I know now. It's like that
show *Entourage*—I did all that and more,' said Philippoussis
in 2010, after discovering that a multi-million-dollar lifestyle
actually costs millions of dollars. 'I just signed on the dotted line
and didn't read the fine print. I didn't understand that maybe
I should ask questions about this or that or check things. It's my
fault, but I didn't know any better, unfortunately.'

It turns out that quite a few players didn't know any
better. Björn Borg, for one. He recently tried to sell all five of
his Wimbledon trophies, plus the Donnay racquet with which he
won one of them. 'He was taken for a big ride,' said tennis writer
Richard Evans, of the star whose sportswear company, Björn Borg
Design, went bankrupt. 'He was much too trusting. He made bad
choices which led to bad luck.'

One of Borg's big rivals, Roscoe Tanner, has also had some bad luck. He keeps getting caught by the police. In and out of court since the end of a tennis career which earned him well over $2 million, the 'chronically broke' former Australian Open champion has been accused of forgery, grand theft and passing dud cheques—and has been jailed many times for failing to pay child support. 'He's stuck in a mind-set where it's still the 1970s and he's winning tournaments,' says Anne Tanner of her father (though behind closed doors, she probably says a lot more).

'I know I let everyone down,' said Tanner in a recent interview, in which he claimed to have turned his life around. 'I didn't represent the sport the way I should have. Getting into the trouble that I've been in, and the things that I've done, I haven't represented the sport well. I'm not proud of myself for that.'

Shortly after the interview, he was arrested for allegedly writing another bad cheque. When this book went to press he was awaiting trial.

But while it doesn't sound like Tanner was much chop as a dad, he was probably better than Peter Graf. The father of tennis legend Steffi famously spent three years in jail after being caught fiddling her taxes. Steffi's finances are very much still intact but it's safe to assume that she now has an accountant.

Aranxta Sánchez Vicario, on the other hand, has a lawyer. And he's been getting a great deal of work. The former Spanish superstar is suing her parents and brother for allegedly siphoning off €16 million of her earnings. 'The relationship with my family is non-existent,' Sanchez Vicario wrote in a recent autobiography. 'How is it possible that everything I obtained has disappeared, does not exist? I am the victim and the cheated one. They have left me with nothing, I'm indebted to the tax office. Now I am without resources. Can I accept this abuse and keep quiet? I'm not going to do so.'

Praising the Lord

Some time after midnight on Sunday 6 January 2013—and not long before the start of the Australian Open—a priest in the remote Melbourne suburb of Greensborough was woken by knocking on his church door. When Father Sipovac opened it, he found himself face to face with the world's best tennis player. Novak Djokovic had driven fifty minutes from his inner-city hotel room to see if a midnight service was being held for the Serbian Orthodox New Year. He was 'crestfallen' to find that the answer was no, so Sipovac held a special service just for him.

'As an athlete and a religious person, it is hard for me to find appropriate words to describe my feelings of gratitude for the confidence I gain from the Holy Synod,' says the Djoker. 'I can only say that it can be earned only with hard work and self-belief, belief in your loved ones and in God.' He was recently awarded the Order of St Sava, the highest honour that can bestowed by the Serbian Orthodox Church.

But the Djoker is far from the only one of today's player to wear a crucifix around their neck on the court. Maria Sharapova, Victoria Azarenka and Juan Martín del Potro also like to remind themselves that Jesus died for their sins, and what better way is there than jewellery?

A T-shirt, perhaps? When Serena Williams claimed Wimbledon in 2012, her father Richard looked on while wearing a T-shirt that said 'Jehovah, my God'. Both Serena and her sister Venus are Jehovah's Witnesses, and both routinely thank The Big Guy whenever they win a tournament—which means that they thank Him rather a lot.

Their boyfriends might not thank Him, though. The Williams sisters don't believe in sex before marriage, and plan to marry men who share their faith. 'I think it's important when you marry to be evenly yoked,' said Serena in an interview with *S2S*.

Marat Safin doesn't ever plan to get married. 'I do not recognise all these formalities. If people love each other, then they don't need these stamps,' he says—and he'd know, because he's loved a lot. The Russian wild man broke over 1000 racquets during the course of his tennis career, and probably as many hearts. If Safin didn't have a busty blonde sitting in his box while he played, that's because he had two or three.

But Safin apparently loves God too. Born and raised a Muslim, he attends prayer sessions in traditional hat and robe, and was recently elected a member of parliament for Vladimir Putin's United Russia party. 'You can't fight your genes,' says the man who's accumulated quite a few fast cars over the years, plus one or two black eyes from brawls. 'I'm Russian, but I'm 100 per cent Muslim. All the Muslim people are passionate, stubborn. We have hot blood.'

I'm not sure what kind of blood Andrea Jaeger has, but it's clear that she has a warm heart. The world number two in 1985, at the crazily young age of sixteen, the American prodigy saw an end to her career at that year's French Open when she popped her right shoulder, and needed a few months out of the game. She could have returned in 1986, but she decided not to. And nor did she pick up a racquet the year after that. Instead, she went and found God. Retreating from the public view, she set up an international charity to help children with cancer—and not long after that, she became a nun.

'My first children's hospital visit was when I was a teenager on the circuit,' says Sister Andrea. 'The kids there had an appreciation of life that I didn't see on the circuit. I had millions of dollars. I had a Mercedes Benz at 17. Who needs a Mercedes Benz at 17? I sold it at 19 and gave the money away and used it to buy toys for kids in hospitals. My parents were shocked. For six months they thought I was joking. I put all my tennis earnings into the foundation. I had enough that I didn't ever have to work again but now I don't have any left.'

God apparently doesn't want Michael Chang to give away all his money. But he was very helpful when it came to winning the French Open. In 1989, the entire tournament 'was really about God wanting a young Chinese boy to win a championship,' says the super-devout Chang, who ends each day with a big bout of Bible-reading, and signs all his autographs 'Jesus loves you'.

'The final with Lendl is evidence of what God can do and [evidence of] His power. Certainly, being 17, I was not expected to win and I wasn't expected to come back from two sets to love down and to do it against Lendl who was a three-time French Open champion. But God has His funny ways of showing His power and He has His funny ways of allowing the weak things of the world to shame the strong.'

This view of the world may meet with God's approval, but for some it was different story. 'He thanks God—credits God—for a win, which offends me,' wrote Andre Agassi in his autobiography. 'That God should take sides in a tennis match, that God should side against me, that God should be in Chang's box, feels ludicrous and insulting.'

'Ludicrous and insulting' are also good words for Margaret Court's post-tennis career. It has seen her put God front and centre—and, of course, far to the right. 'Homosexuality is an abomination to the Lord! Abortion is an abomination to the Lord!' proclaims the former superstar, who became a Pentecostal minister in the mid-1990s.

'I was just standing in the kitchen doing the dishes and it was around dinner time and just all of a sudden, I had a great impression. I just felt God was speaking to me, and it was through the power of the Holy Spirit. I just knew somehow I'd be starting a church.'

Oh God, when will this end?

THE GRAND PRIZES

Before players walk into centre court at Wimbledon, they see a famous quote from Rudyard Kipling, inscribed on the wall just above the door: 'If you can meet with triumph and disaster, and treat those two imposters just the same.'

Taken from his famous poem 'If' — a paean to the stiff upper lip — the lines are supposed to remind us that winning isn't everything (and, no, it's not 'the only thing' either).

Kipling's right, dammit, and this book has got it all wrong. Apologies for writing it and all that, but you should really blame the publisher: I'm just their pawn. For 160 pages now, we've just been focusing on who's good at tennis: who's had a good forehand, a good backhand, and good serve. But what about all the other good stuff out there? What about all the good tennis stories that I haven't had a chance to squeeze in?

It's time, then, to award the grand prizes. Let's take a moment to celebrate all those little things that make the game matter such a lot.

The most committed tennis fan

Surf the web for a tennis fan site, and you'll very soon be drowning in love. 'The best moment of my life just happened!' blogs 'Laurence', after posting a selfie with Maria Sharapova. 'I feel constant surprise, joy, and elation,' is 'Anna's' contribution to a discussion about Novak Djokovic. For 'shazadtheprince', meanwhile, Roger Federer 'is an inspiration ... I can't thank

him enough for what he has given to us fans and to the tennis ...
He is tennis history's true hero.'

But talk is cheap, my friends. The prize for *true* fandom goes to middle-aged stalker William Lepeska, a man who spent five years being obsessed with Mel B of the Spice Girls before he 'finally said to heck with her and moved on to greener pastures'. Those pastures involved getting the name Anna Kournikova tattooed on his arm, and bombarding its owner with letters and emails.

When Anna, for some reason, failed to reply to them, Lepeska took the hint. He stripped off all his clothes and swam 300 metres across Biscayne Bay in order to visit the Russian's home in Miami Beach. A good plan with one slight problem. He turned up at the wrong house.

The least committed tennis fan

It's tempting to give this award to US President Barack Obama, the man who converted the White House's century-old tennis court into (sigh) a place to play basketball.

But there's no going past Christina Aguilera, a singer who once met Tiger Woods. 'Christina, I love your music,' the golfer told her, politely. 'I have all your CDs ...'

'Sorry, I don't follow tennis,' Aguilera replied, 'so I don't know much about you.'

The best coulda-been champion

There are a few contenders for this one. David Foster Wallace, for example, was a 'near great'—at least, according to him. But according to the rankings, the author of *Infinite Jest* was actually just the eleventh best junior player in central Illinois.

In the TV world, *Friends* star Matthew Perry was a nationally ranked junior. Though on the other hand, his nation was Canada.

'I was a very good tennis player in Ottawa ... then I moved to Los Angeles when I was 15, and everyone in L.A. just killed me ... Giving up tennis wasn't really a decision I had to make.'

The Big Bang Theory's Kaley Cuoco is another coulda-been champ. 'Penny' was America's fifty-fourth best thirteen-year-old, before she gave the game away to act full-time.

But I think that the prize should go to someone who's *never* given the game away—to a celebrity who could still be. Redfoo, take a bow. The thirty-seven-year-old singer is still plugging away at his pro tennis career, despite being a thirty-seven-year-old singer. He spent much of 2013 and 2014 trying to qualify for the US Open, and is reportedly planning to waste 2015 as well.

The worst doubles team

Hands down, this prize goes to Mark Philippoussis and Goran Ivanisevic. Or maybe that should be 'heads down'. The pair came together to play a doubles match in the late 1990s, but at one point they came a little too close. The Aussie was concussed when pair banged heads at the net, while the Croat needed half a dozen stitches.

The best name

This award category offers a lot of scope for potty humour, but I'm certainly not going to take it. It would be very easy to mention Max Cocks, for example, and make some tawdry gag about how he should meet Nungnadda Wannasuk, or the American player Happy Ho. But don't worry, there'll be none of that smut here. You won't see me write the names Hana Fukarkova and Olga Khrapkova either, let alone Martine Poos.

So let's just give the prize to Anna Smashnova. Now *there's* a great name for a tennis player. Holy cow, as Holly Cao might say.

The most inappropriate interview

It's hard to know who's more to blame for the below interview: *We are Tennis*, the European website that asked the questions, or Benoît Paire, the French player who answered them? So let's be fair and blame them both.

▸ What do you first look at [when you see] a girl who's beautiful inside?
Her bum.

▸ How do you recognise fake tits from real ones?
A little scar a little under them but, well, you have to be a bit of an expert. I'm not a fan of big tits; I'm more into small ones, preferably natural.

▸ Do you prefer going out with a bearded woman or a humpback woman?
A humpback woman.

▸ If you could spend one day with Pamela Anderson, what would you do?
I would take advantage of it to get into her tits. To know them.

▸ What do you do if your wife disobeys you?
I hit her. No, I'm just kidding of course. We would have sex right away.

▸ What's the purpose of Benedict XVI's penis?
To pee.

▸ Would you have sex with a member of your family to save him?
Never!

The best scientific research

I don't know who hands out the Nobel Prize for Physiology, but I do know that they get it all wrong. Instead of awarding it to people like Professors Christiane Nüsslein-Volhard and Eric F Wieschaus 'for their discoveries concerning the genetic control of early embryonic development', they should have given it to that guy who took part in a science experiment by placing a tennis ball machine right in front of his crotch.

Several agonising minutes later, an important discovery was made. Whenever the machine was turned on, the guy's pulse rate increased quite a bit.

The worst scientific research

Midway through the summer of 2007—just a few short years into the War on Terror—a state park in Athens, Georgia, was closed to visitors for several days. The measure was taken after a visitor saw a suspicious-looking individual place six tennis balls in the park's lake—all of which almost immediately sank.

'The balls sank rather than floating,' a vigilant government official told the assembled media throng. 'It was further observed that the tennis balls contained an unknown substance.'

Poison? Nuclear waste? Some kind of explosive? After rigorous tests were carried out, it was found that the balls did indeed contain a foreign substance.

Water.

The best tennis diet

If you really are what you eat, then Patty Schnyder is basically orange juice. The recently retired Swiss player—a one-time world number seven—used to get by on 3 litres a day of the stuff, on the advice of her boyfriend, a 'natural therapist' some decades her senior. A man who claimed to have discovered the cure for cancer (and, in his spare time, a cure for AIDS), Rainer Harnecker also liked to treat the nineteen-year-old's injuries with hot wax, and a rolling pin covered in needles.

The player's parents seem to have had one or two doubts about Harnecker, and hired a detective to investigate his methods, with mixed results. On the one hand, the couple broke up. But on the other, Schnyder became engaged to the detective ... a man who was shortly afterwards found guilty of fraud.

The worst training method

Yevgeny Kafelnikov was fond of the punching bag—but it wasn't so fond of him. The Russian withdrew from the 1997 Australian Open, and spent a further three months on the tennis sidelines, after some slightly overeager punching saw him break his hand.

The best victory celebration

This prize ought to belong to the 2006 US Open winner Maria Sharapova. She raised the big silver trophy aloft to the crowd ... only for the lid to fall off and crash onto her head.

But I just can't go past Tamarine Tanasugarn's victory dance at the same tournament, in a third round match in 2003. She let out a loud shriek on match point, acknowledged the crowd and went to the net for a handshake. Only to be informed that it wasn't match point.

The worst victory celebration

This one goes to Pete Sampras, for his win over Andrei Chesnokov in the 1995 Davis Cup final. 'We were battling in a five-set match and I finally got to match point. I ended up winning the long point and raised my hands in victory and completely collapsed with cramps in my legs. I couldn't walk off the court and had to be carried off by our team trainer and doctor.'

The best death threat

This may be one of our tackier categories, but what the hell, let's push on. The grand prize goes to an anonymous blogger known as 'Blue Cat Polytheistic Religion Founder 07', but let's call him 'Blue' for short. In late September 2012, Blue posted the following message on a Chinese website, in reference to the upcoming Shanghai Masters: 'On October 6, I plan to assassinate Federer for the purpose of tennis extermination.' The post was accompanied by a doctored image of a decapitated Federer on his knees on a tennis court, with an executioner holding an axe nearby.

Tournament organisers and police spent the next week on high alert, while the normally unflappable Federer was about as flapped as he's ever been. 'Obviously maybe it's a little bit of a distraction, there's no doubt about it. But you have to be aware of what's happening around you. But that is the case anyway anywhere I go today with my fame and all that stuff.'

In the end, nothing actually happened to him, and the still-anonymous blogger posted a humble apology.

The most inappropriate tennis court

Federer and Agassi got plenty of headlines when they played an exhibition match on top of the Burj Al Arab—at 321 metres, the world's third-tallest hotel. But that match was no match for the one in 1925 that took place on an aeroplane. While it was up in the air.

The most inappropriate tennis rule

When Wimbledon officials say that they want players to wear all-white, they really mean *all*-white. According to *The Telegraph*, a recent clampdown of clothing regulations has meant that some female players have been forced to play without a bra because the one that they brought was too dark.

The biggest tennis mystery

In 1424 tennis was banned from the streets of Atherstone, in Warwickshire, according to a document recently uncovered in Britain's national archives. Exactly why, we'll probably never know.

But as mysteries go, the ban pales in comparison to The Adventure of the Ball-Blocked Sewer, which took place in Leicestershire in early 2014. When a large sewer in that small county kept on flooding, some engineers were call in to uncover why. The reason, they found, was that it was blocked with hundreds and hundreds of tennis balls. Even though a tennis court was nowhere in sight.

The best sewer story

See above.

The most lethal serve

Stefan Edberg had a great serve, but it would be tactless to call it a lethal one.

However, it would also be accurate. During a Junior Boys' Title Match at the 1983 US Open, when the future Swedish star was just sixteen years old, he mis-hit a serve straight into the groin of a linesman who was sitting on a chair by the court. The blow knocked sixty-one-year-old Dick Wertheim backwards. He struck his head, and was rushed to hospital.

A week later he was taken to the cemetery.

The best transgender contender

This prize goes to Renée Richards. Or Richard Raskind, as she was once known.

A Yale-educated ophthalmologist from New York City, Richards was a good but not quite pro-standard tennis player during the days that her passport said 'male'. But after she underwent gender reassignment surgery in 1975, at the tender age of forty-one, she suddenly found herself a world-class player—if only the WTA would allow her to play.

Richards was barred from competing in Grand Slams in the summer of 1976, but successfully overturned the ban in the New York Supreme Court. She played professionally from 1977 until 1981, when she retired at forty-seven without winning a tournament. But she did make the doubles final of one US Open, scoring a victory on behalf of transgender athletes all over the globe.

The best wig story

Tennis at the highest level is as much a mind game as anything else. Letting your attention wander even for a moment can very easily mean game, set and match.

Andre Agassi may just have neglected this rule during his first ever Grand Slam final. The balding star had recently started wearing a wig, both on court and in the shower. But the night before the final, as Agassi stood under the shower, he realised his wig was falling apart.

Panicking, he had his brother clamp it back on with hair clips.

'Do you think it will hold?'

'Just don't move so much.'

'Of course I could have played without my hairpiece,' the man for whom 'Image is everything' later wrote, 'but what would all the journalists have written if they knew that all the time I was really wearing a wig? During the warming-up training before play I prayed. Not for victory, but that my hairpiece would not fall off. With each leap, I imagined it falling into the sand. I imagined millions of spectators move closer to their TV sets, their eyes widening and, in dozens of dialects and languages, ask how Andre Agassi's hair has fallen from his head.'

He lost.

The worst tennis trophy

Once upon a time, in the good old days, when life was simple and the world was young, a trophy was just a trophy. Just a big, shiny silver cup. A tennis player got it if he or she won a tournament, then gave it pride of place on the mantlepiece at home.

You'd have to suspect that some of today's trophies go right into the bin. Arty types have become involved in the process, and unfortunately we can't have them all shot. Just witness the dismay of Acapulco Open winners when they are awarded a large metal pear, or the shame on the face of Sydney International winners when they are handed a sort of big disco ball. The winners of the Atlanta Open are rewarded with an ugly red vase; the winners of the German Open with something that looks like a fan. The Paris Masters hands out a sort of misshapen tree, the Portugal Open some hideous pottery.

But *our* prize goes to the Madrid Masters. Its trophy looks like a dildo.

The best tennis quotes

Honourable mentions go to Mitch Hedberg—'The depressing thing about tennis is that no matter how good I get, I'll never be as good as a wall'—and the ever-reliable Anonymous—'To err is human. To put the blame on someone else is doubles.'

But the grand prize goes to a triumphant Vitas Gerulaitis, after he mustered up his first ever win against Jimmy Connors: 'Nobody beats Vitas Gerulaitis 17 times in a row.'

The worst tennis quote

'Tennis: the most perfect combination of athleticism, artistry, power, style, and wit. A beautiful game, but one so remorselessly travestied by the passage of time.' Thanks for that, Martin 'Pretentious Git' Amis.

The best tennis joke

Q: Why is a tennis game a noisy game?
A: Because each player raises a racket.

The second-best tennis joke

Q: Why should you never fall in love with a tennis player?
A: To them, 'love' means nothing.

The worst tennis joke

Q: What did one tennis ball say to the other tennis ball?
A: 'See you round.'

The best line to end a tennis book with

'The end.' Actually, no scrap that. Let's go with ...

Game, set and match.

ROLL OF HONOUR

There are lies, damned lies and statistics, as the English prime minister Benjamin Disraeli once said. Though according to some sources, this is itself a damned lie, as the phrase was actually said by Mark Twain.

Anyway, here are some statistics. I got them from Wikipedia, so fingers crossed.

Wimbledon – Gentlemen's Singles

1877	Spencer Gore GBR
1878	Frank Hadow GBR
1879	John Hartley GBR
1880	John Hartley GBR
1881	William Renshaw GBR
1882	William Renshaw GBR
1883	William Renshaw GBR
1884	William Renshaw GBR
1885	William Renshaw GBR
1886	William Renshaw GBR
1887	Herbert Lawford GBR
1888	Ernest Renshaw GBR
1889	William Renshaw GBR
1890	Willoughby Hamilton GBR
1891	Wilfred Baddeley GBR
1892	Wilfred Baddeley GBR
1893	Joshua Pim GBR
1894	Joshua Pim GBR
1895	Wilfred Baddeley GBR
1896	Harold Mahony GBR
1897	Reginald Doherty GBR
1898	Reginald Doherty GBR

1899	Reginald Doherty GBR
1900	Reginald Doherty GBR
1901	Arthur Gore GBR
1902	Laurence Doherty GBR
1903	Laurence Doherty GBR
1904	Laurence Doherty GBR
1905	Laurence Doherty GBR
1906	Laurence Doherty GBR
1907	Norman Brookes AUS
1908	Arthur Gore GBR
1909	Arthur Gore GBR
1910	Tony Wilding NZL
1911	Tony Wilding NZL
1912	Tony Wilding NZL
1913	Tony Wilding NZL
1914	Norman Brookes AUS
1915–18	*No competition*
1919	Gerald Patterson AUS
1920	Bill Tilden USA
1921	Bill Tilden USA
1922	Gerald Patterson AUS
1923	Bill Johnston USA
1924	Jean Borotra FRA
1925	René Lacoste FRA
1926	Jean Borotra FRA
1927	Henri Cochet FRA
1928	René Lacoste FRA
1929	Henri Cochet FRA
1930	Bill Tilden USA
1931	Sidney Wood USA
1932	Elsworth Vines USA
1933	Jack Crawford AUS
1934	Fred Perry GBR

1935	Fred Perry GBR
1936	Fred Perry GBR
1937	Don Budge USA
1938	Don Budge USA
1939	Bobby Riggs USA
1940–45	*No competition*
1946	Yvon Petra FRA
1947	Jack Kramer USA
1948	Bob Falkenburg USA
1949	Ted Schroeder USA
1950	Budge Patty USA
1951	Dick Savitt USA
1952	Frank Sedgman AUS
1953	Vic Seixas USA
1954	Jaroslav Drobný EGY
1955	Tony Trabert USA
1956	Lew Hoad AUS
1957	Lew Hoad AUS
1958	Ashley Cooper AUS
1959	Alex Olmedo USA
1960	Neale Fraser AUS
1961	Rod Laver AUS
1962	Rod Laver AUS
1963	Chuck McKinley USA
1964	Roy Emerson AUS
1965	Roy Emerson AUS
1966	Manuel Santana ESP
1967	John Newcombe AUS
1968	Rod Laver AUS
1969	Rod Laver AUS
1970	John Newcombe AUS
1971	John Newcombe AUS
1972	Stan Smith USA

1973	Jan Kodeš CZE
1974	Jimmy Connors USA
1975	Arthur Ashe USA
1976	Björn Borg SWE
1977	Björn Borg SWE
1978	Björn Borg SWE
1979	Björn Borg SWE
1980	Björn Borg SWE
1981	John McEnroe USA
1982	Jimmy Connors USA
1983	John McEnroe USA
1984	John McEnroe USA
1985	Boris Becker GER
1986	Boris Becker GER
1987	Pat Cash AUS
1988	Stefan Edberg SWE
1989	Boris Becker GER
1990	Stefan Edberg SWE
1991	Michael Stich GER
1992	Andre Agassi USA
1993	Pete Sampras USA
1994	Pete Sampras USA
1995	Pete Sampras USA
1996	Richard Krajicek NED
1997	Pete Sampras USA
1998	Pete Sampras USA
1999	Pete Sampras USA
2000	Pete Sampras USA
2001	Goran Ivanisevic CRO
2002	Lleyton Hewitt AUS
2003	Roger Federer SUI
2004	Roger Federer SUI
2005	Roger Federer SUI

2006	Roger Federer SUI
2007	Roger Federer SUI
2008	Rafael Nadal ESP
2009	Roger Federer SUI
2010	Rafael Nadal ESP
2011	Novak Djokovic SRB
2012	Roger Federer SUI
2013	Andy Murray GBR

Wimbledon – Ladies' Singles

1884	Maud Watson GBR
1885	Maud Watson GBR
1886	Blanche Bingley GBR
1887	Lottie Dod GBR
1888	Lottie Dod GBR
1889	Blanche Hillyard GBR
1890	Lena Rice GBR
1891	Lottie Dod GBR
1892	Lottie Dod GBR
1893	Lottie Dod GBR
1894	Blanche Hillyard GBR
1895	Charlotte Cooper GBR
1896	Charlotte Cooper GBR
1897	Blanche Hillyard GBR
1898	Charlotte Cooper GBR
1899	Blanche Hillyard GBR
1900	Blanche Hillyard GBR
1901	Charlotte Sterry GBR
1902	Muriel Robb GBR
1903	Dorothea Douglass GBR
1904	Dorothea Douglass GBR
1905	May Sutton USA
1906	Dorothea Douglass GBR
1907	May Sutton USA

1908	Charlotte Sterry GBR
1909	Dora Boothby GBR
1910	Dorothea Chambers GBR
1911	Dorothea Chambers GBR
1912	Ethel Larcombe GBR
1913	Dorothea Chambers GBR
1914	Dorothea Chambers GBR
1915–18	*No competition*
1919	Suzanne Lenglen FRA
1920	Suzanne Lenglen FRA
1921	Suzanne Lenglen FRA
1922	Suzanne Lenglen FRA
1923	Suzanne Lenglen FRA
1924	Kitty Godfree GBR
1925	Suzanne Lenglen FRA
1926	Kitty Godfree GBR
1927	Helen Wills USA
1928	Helen Wills USA
1929	Helen Wills USA
1930	Helen Wills USA
1931	Cilly Aussem GER
1932	Helen Wills USA
1933	Helen Wills USA
1934	Dorothy Round GBR
1935	Helen Wills USA
1936	Helen Jacobs USA
1937	Dorothy Round GBR
1938	Helen Wills USA
1939	Alice Marble USA
1940–45	*No competition*
1946	Pauline Betz USA
1947	Margaret Osborne USA
1948	Louise Brough USA

1949	Louise Brough USA
1950	Louise Brough USA
1951	Doris Hart USA
1952	Maureen Connolly USA
1953	Maureen Connolly USA
1954	Maureen Connolly USA
1955	Louise Brough USA
1956	Shirley Fry USA
1957	Althea Gibson USA
1958	Althea Gibson USA
1959	Maria Bueno BRA
1960	Maria Bueno BRA
1961	Angela Mortimer GBR
1962	Karen Susman USA
1963	Margaret Court AUS
1964	Maria Bueno BRA
1965	Margaret Court AUS
1966	Billie Jean King USA
1967	Billie Jean King USA
1968	Billie Jean King USA
1969	Ann Jones GBR
1970	Margaret Court AUS
1971	Evonne Goolagong AUS
1972	Billie Jean King USA
1973	Billie Jean King USA
1974	Chris Evert USA
1975	Billie Jean King USA
1976	Chris Evert USA
1977	Virginia Wade GBR
1978	Martina Navratilova USA
1979	Martina Navratilova USA
1980	Evonne Goolagong AUS
1981	Chris Evert USA

1982	Martina Navratilova USA
1983	Martina Navratilova USA
1984	Martina Navratilova USA
1985	Martina Navratilova USA
1986	Martina Navratilova USA
1987	Martina Navratilova USA
1988	Steffi Graf GER
1989	Steffi Graf GER
1990	Martina Navratilova USA
1991	Steffi Graf GER
1992	Steffi Graf GER
1993	Steffi Graf GER
1994	Conchita Martínez ESP
1995	Steffi Graf GER
1996	Steffi Graf GER
1997	Martina Hingis SUI
1998	Jana Novotná CZE
1999	Lindsay Davenport USA
2000	Venus Williams USA
2001	Venus Williams USA
2002	Serena Williams USA
2003	Serena Williams USA
2004	Maria Sharapova RUS
2005	Venus Williams USA
2006	Amélie Mauresmo FRA
2007	Venus Williams USA
2008	Venus Williams USA
2009	Serena Williams USA
2010	Serena Williams USA
2011	Petra Kvitová CZE
2012	Serena Williams USA
2013	Marion Bartoli FRA
2014	Petra Kvitová CZE

US Open – Men's Singles

1881	Richard Sears USA
1882	Richard Sears USA
1883	Richard Sears USA
1884	Richard Sears USA
1885	Richard Sears USA
1886	Richard Sears USA
1887	Richard Sears USA
1888	Henry Slocum, Jr USA
1889	Henry Slocum, Jr USA
1890	Oliver Campbell USA
1891	Oliver Campbell USA
1892	Oliver Campbell USA
1893	Robert Wrenn USA
1894	Robert Wrenn USA
1895	Fred H Hovey USA
1896	Robert Wrenn USA
1897	Robert Wrenn USA
1898	Malcolm Whitman USA
1899	Malcolm Whitman USA
1900	Malcolm Whitman USA
1901	William Larned USA
1902	William Larned USA
1903	Laurence Dohesty GBR
1904	Holcombe Ward USA
1905	Beals Wright USA
1906	William Larned USA
1907	William Larned USA
1908	William Larned USA
1909	William Larned USA
1910	William Larned USA
1911	William Larned USA
1912	Maurice McLoughlin USA

1913	Maurice McLoughlin USA
1914	Richard Williams USA
1915	William Johnston USA
1916	Richard Williams USA
1917	R Lindley Murray USA
1918	R Lindley Murray USA
1919	William Johnston USA
1920	Bill Tilden USA
1921	Bill Tilden USA
1922	Bill Tilden USA
1923	Bill Tilden USA
1924	Bill Tilden USA
1925	Bill Tilden USA
1926	René Lacoste FRA
1927	René Lacoste FRA
1928	Henri Cochet FRA
1929	Bill Tilden USA
1930	John Doeg USA
1931	Ellsworth Vines USA
1932	Ellsworth Vines USA
1933	Fred Perry GBR
1934	Fred Perry GBR
1935	Wilmer Allison USA
1936	Fred Perry GBR
1937	Don Budge USA
1938	Don Budge USA
1939	Bobby Riggs USA
1940	Donald McNeill USA
1941	Bobby Riggs USA
1942	Fred Schroeder, Jr USA
1943	Lt Joseph Hunt USA
1944	Sgt Frank Parker USA
1945	Sgt Frank Parker USA

1946	Jack Kramer AUS
1947	Jack Kramer AUS
1948	Richard Gonzales USA
1949	Richard Gonzales USA
1950	Arthur Larsen USA
1951	Frank Sedgman AUS
1952	Frank Sedgman AUS
1953	Tony Trabert USA
1954	Vic Seixas USA
1955	Tony Trabert USA
1956	Ken Rosewall AUS
1957	Malcolm Anderson AUS
1958	Ashley J Cooper AUS
1959	Neale Fraser AUS
1960	Neale Fraser AUS
1961	Roy Emerson AUS
1962	Rod Laver AUS
1963	Rafael Osuna MEX
1964	Roy Emerson AUS
1965	Manuel Santana ESP
1966	Fred Stolle AUS
1967	John Newcombe AUS
1968	Arthur Ashe USA
1969	Rod Laver AUS
1970	Ken Rosewall AUS
1971	Stan Smith USA
1972	Ilie Năstase ROU
1973	John Newcombe AUS
1974	Jimmy Connors USA
1975	Manuel Orantes USA
1976	Jimmy Connors USA
1977	Guillermo Vilas USA
1978	Jimmy Connors USA

1979	John McEnroe USA
1980	John McEnroe USA
1981	John McEnroe USA
1982	Jimmy Connors USA
1983	Jimmy Connors USA
1984	John McEnroe USA
1985	Ivan Lendl CZE
1986	Ivan Lendl CZE
1987	Ivan Lendl CZE
1988	Mats Wilander SWE
1989	Boris Becker GER
1990	Pete Sampras USA
1991	Stefan Edberg SWE
1992	Stefan Edberg SWE
1993	Pete Sampras USA
1994	Andre Agassi USA
1995	Pete Sampras USA
1996	Pete Sampras USA
1997	Patrick Rafter AUS
1998	Patrick Rafter AUS
1999	Andre Agassi USA
2000	Marat Safin RUS
2001	Lleyton Hewitt AUS
2002	Pete Sampras USA
2003	Andy Roddick USA
2004	Roger Federer SUI
2005	Roger Federer SUI
2006	Roger Federer SUI
2007	Roger Federer SUI
2008	Roger Federer SUI
2009	Juan Martín del Potro ARG
2010	Rafael Nadal ESP
2011	Novak Djokovic SRB

2012	Andy Murray GBR
2013	Rafael Nadal ESP
2014	Marin Čilić CRO

US Open – Women's Singles

1887	Ellen Hansell USA
1888	Bertha Townsend USA
1889	Bertha Townsend USA
1890	Ellen Roosevelt USA
1891	Mabel Cahill GBR
1892	Mabel Cahill GBR
1893	Aline Terry USA
1894	Helen Hellwig USA
1895	Juliette Atkinson USA
1896	Elisabeth Moore USA
1897	Juliette Atkinson USA
1898	Juliette Atkinson USA
1899	Marion Jones USA
1900	Myrtle McAteer USA
1901	Elisabeth Moore USA
1902	Marion Jones USA
1903	Elisabeth Moore USA
1904	May Sutton USA
1905	Elisabeth Moore USA
1906	Helen Homans USA
1907	Evelyn Sears USA
1908	Maud Barger-Wallach USA
1909	Hazel Hotchkiss USA
1910	Hazel Hotchkiss USA
1911	Hazel Hotchkiss USA
1912	Mary Browne USA
1913	Mary Browne USA
1914	Mary Browne USA
1915	Molla Bjurstedt NOR

1916	Molla Bjurstedt NOR
1917	Molla Bjurstedt NOR
1918	Molla Bjurstedt NOR
1919	Hazel Hotchkiss Wightman
1920	Molla B Mallory
1921	Molla B Mallory
1922	Molla B Mallory
1923	Helen Wills USA
1924	Helen Wills USA
1925	Helen Wills USA
1926	Molla B Mallory
1927	Helen Wills USA
1928	Helen Wills USA
1929	Helen Wills USA
1930	Betty Nuthall GBR
1931	Helen Wills USA
1932	Helen Jacobs USA
1933	Helen Jacobs USA
1934	Helen Jacobs USA
1935	Helen Jacobs USA
1936	Alice Marble USA
1937	Anita Lizana CHI
1938	Alice Marble USA
1939	Alice Marble USA
1940	Alice Marble USA
1941	Sarah Palfrey Cooke USA
1942	Pauline Betz USA
1943	Pauline Betz USA
1944	Pauline Betz USA
1945	Sarah Palfrey Cooke USA
1946	Pauline Betz USA
1947	Louise Brough USA
1948	Margaret Osborne duPont USA

1949	Margaret Osborne duPont USA
1950	Margaret Osborne duPont USA
1951	Maureen Connolly USA
1952	Maureen Connolly USA
1953	Maureen Connolly USA
1954	Doris Hart USA
1955	Doris Hart USA
1956	Shirley J Fry USA
1957	Althea Gibson USA
1958	Althea Gibson USA
1959	Maria Bueno BRA
1960	Darlene Hard USA
1961	Darlene Hard USA
1962	Margaret Court AUS
1963	Maria Bueno BRA
1964	Maria Bueno BRA
1965	Margaret Court AUS
1966	Maria Bueno BRA
1967	Billie Jean King USA
1968	Virginia Wade GBR
1969	Margaret Court AUS
1970	Margaret Court AUS
1971	Billie Jean King USA
1972	Billie Jean King USA
1973	Margaret Court AUS
1974	Billie Jean King USA
1975	Chris Evert USA
1976	Chris Evert USA
1977	Chris Evert USA
1978	Chris Evert USA
1979	Tracy Austin USA
1980	Chris Evert USA
1981	Tracy Austin USA

1982	Chris Evert USA
1983	Martina Navratilova USA
1984	Martina Navratilova USA
1985	Hana Mandlíková USA
1986	Martina Navratilova USA
1987	Martina Navratilova USA
1988	Steffi Graf GER
1989	Steffi Graf GER
1990	Gabriela Sabatini ARG
1991	Monica Seles YUG
1992	Monica Seles YUG
1993	Steffi Graf GER
1994	Aranxta Sánchez Vicario ESP
1995	Steffi Graf GER
1996	Steffi Graf GER
1997	Martina Hingis SUI
1998	Lindsay Davenport USA
1999	Serena Williams USA
2000	Venus Williams USA
2001	Venus Williams USA
2002	Serena Williams USA
2003	Justine Henin BEL
2004	Svetlana Kuznetsova RUS
2005	Kim Clijsters BEL
2006	Maria Sharapova
2007	Justine Henin BEL
2008	Serena Williams USA
2009	Kim Clijsters BEL
2010	Kim Clijsters BEL
2011	Samantha Stosur AUS
2012	Serena Williams USA
2013	Serena Williams USA
2014	Serena Williams USA

French Open – Men's Singles

1891	H Briggs GBR
1892	J Schopfer FRA
1893	L Riboulet FRA
1894	André Vacherot FRA
1895	André Vacherot FRA
1896	André Vacherot FRA
1897	Paul Aymé FRA
1898	Paul Aymé FRA
1899	Paul Aymé FRA
1900	Paul Aymé FRA
1901	André Vacherot FRA
1902	Marcel Vacherot FRA
1903	Max Decugis FRA
1904	Max Decugis FRA
1905	Maurice Germot FRA
1906	Maurice Germot FRA
1907	Max Decugis FRA
1908	Max Decugis FRA
1909	Max Decugis FRA
1910	Maurice Germot FRA
1911	André Gobert FRA
1912	Max Decugis FRA
1913	Max Decugis FRA
1914	Max Decugis FRA
1915–19	*No competition*
1920	André Gobert FRA
1921	Jean-Pierre Samazeuilh FRA
1922	Henri Cochet FRA
1923	François Blanchy FRA
1924	Jean Borotra FRA
1925	René Lacoste FRA
1926	Henri Cochet FRA

1927	René Lacoste FRA
1928	Henri Cochet FRA
1929	René Lacoste FRA
1930	Henri Cochet FRA
1931	Jean Borotra FRA
1932	Henri Cochet FRA
1933	John Crawford AUS
1934	Gottfried Von Cramm GER
1935	Fred Perry GBR
1936	Gottfried Von Cramm GER
1937	Henner Henkel GER
1938	Donald Budge USA
1939	William McNeill USA
1940–45	*No competition*
1946	Marcel Bernard FRA
1947	József Asbóth HUN
1948	Frank Parker USA
1949	Frank Parker USA
1950	Budge Patty USA
1951	Jaroslav Drobný CZE
1952	Jaroslav Drobný CZE
1953	Ken Rosewall AUS
1954	Tony Trabert USA
1955	Tony Trabert USA
1956	Lewis Hoad AUS
1957	Sven Davidson SWE
1958	Mervyn Rose AUS
1959	Nicola Pietrangeli ITA
1960	Nicola Pietrangeli ITA
1961	Manuel Santana ESP
1962	Rod Laver AUS
1963	Roy Emerson AUS
1964	Manuel Santana ESP

1965	Fred Stolle AUS
1966	Tony Roche AUS
1967	Roy Emerson AUS
1968	Ken Rosewall AUS
1969	Rod Laver AUS
1970	Jan Kodeš CZE
1971	Jan Kodeš CZE
1972	Andrés Gimeno ESP
1973	Ilie Năstase ROM
1974	Björn Borg SWE
1975	Björn Borg SWE
1976	Adriano Panatta ITA
1977	Guillermo Vilas ARG
1978	Björn Borg SWE
1979	Björn Borg SWE
1980	Björn Borg SWE
1981	Björn Borg SWE
1982	Mats Wilander SWE
1983	Yannick Noah FRA
1984	Ivan Lendl CZE
1985	Mats Wilander SWE
1986	Ivan Lendl CZE
1987	Ivan Lendl CZE
1988	Mats Wilander SWE
1989	Michael Chang USA
1990	Andrés Gómez ECU
1991	Jim Courier USA
1992	Jim Courier USA
1993	Sergi Bruguera ESP
1994	Sergi Bruguera ESP
1995	Thomas Muster AUT
1996	Yevgeny Kafelnikov RUS
1997	Gustavo Kuerten BRA

ROLL OF HONOUR

1998	Carlos Moyá ESP
1999	Andre Agassi USA
2000	Gustavo Kuerten BRA
2001	Gustavo Kuerten BRA
2002	Albert Costa ESP
2003	Juan Carlos Ferrero ESP
2004	Gastón Gaudio ARG
2005	Rafael Nadal ESP
2006	Rafael Nadal ESP
2007	Rafael Nadal ESP
2008	Rafael Nadal ESP
2009	Roger Federer SUI
2010	Rafael Nadal ESP
2011	Rafael Nadal ESP
2012	Rafael Nadal ESP
2013	Rafael Nadal ESP

French Open – Women's Singles

1897	Adine Masson FRA
1898	Adine Masson FRA
1899	Adine Masson FRA
1900	Hélène Prévost FRA
1901	P Girod FRA
1902	Adine Masson FRA
1903	Adine Masson FRA
1904	Kate Gillou FRA
1905	Kate Gillou FRA
1906	Kate Gillou-Fenwick FRA
1907	Comtesse de Kermel FRA
1908	Kate Gillou-Fenwick FRA
1909	Jeanne Matthey FRA
1910	Jeanne Matthey FRA
1911	Jeanne Matthey FRA
1912	Jeanne Matthey FRA

1913	Marguerite Broquedis FRA
1914	Marguerite Broquedis FRA
1915–19	*No competition*
1920	Suzanne Lenglen FRA
1921	Suzanne Lenglen FRA
1922	Suzanne Lenglen FRA
1923	Suzanne Lenglen FRA
1924	Diddie Vlasto FRA
1925	Suzanne Lenglen FRA
1926	Suzanne Lenglen FRA
1927	Kornelia Bouman NED
1928	Helen Wills USA
1929	Helen Wills USA
1930	Helen Wills-Moody USA
1931	Cilly Aussem GER
1932	Helen Wills-Moody USA
1933	Margaret Scriven GBR
1934	Margaret Scriven GBR
1935	Hilde Sperling GER
1936	Hilde Sperling GER
1937	Hilde Sperling GER
1938	Simone Mathieu FRA
1939	Simone Mathieu FRA
1940–45	*No competition*
1946	Margaret Osborne USA
1947	Patricia Todd USA
1948	Nelly Landry FRA
1949	Margaret Osborne duPont USA
1950	Doris Hart USA
1951	Shirley Fry USA
1952	Doris Hart USA
1953	Maureen Connolly USA
1954	Maureen Connolly USA

1955	Angela Mortimer	GBR
1956	Althea Gibson	USA
1957	Shirley Bloomer	GBR
1958	Zsuzsi Körmöczy	HUN
1959	Christine Truman	GBR
1960	Darlene Hard	USA
1961	Ann Haydon	GBR
1962	Margaret Smith	AUS
1963	Lesley Turner	AUS
1964	Margaret Smith	AUS
1965	Lesley Turner	AUS
1966	Ann Haydon-Jones	GBR
1967	Françoise Dürr	FRA
1968	Nancy Richey	USA
1969	Margaret Smith-Court	AUS
1970	Margaret Smith-Court	AUS
1971	Evonne Goolagong	AUS
1972	Billie-Jean King	USA
1973	Margaret Smith-Court	AUS
1974	Chris Evert	USA
1975	Chris Evert	USA
1976	Sue Barker	GBR
1977	Mima Jaušovec	YUG
1978	Virginia Ruzici	ROM
1979	Chris Evert-Lloyd	USA
1980	Chris Evert-Lloyd	USA
1981	Hana Mandlíková	CZE
1982	Martina Navratilova	USA
1983	Chris Evert-Lloyd	USA
1984	Martina Navratilova	USA
1985	Chris Evert-Lloyd	USA
1986	Chris Evert-Lloyd	USA
1987	Steffi Graf	GER

1988	Steffi Graf GER
1989	Arantxa Sánchez Vicario ESP
1990	Monica Seles YUG
1991	Monica Seles YUG
1992	Monica Seles YUG
1993	Steffi Graf GER
1994	Arantxa Sánchez Vicario ESP
1995	Steffi Graf GER
1996	Steffi Graf GER
1997	Iva Majoli CRO
1998	Arantxa Sánchez Vicario ESP
1999	Steffi Graf GER
2000	Mary Pierce FRA
2001	Jennifer Capriati USA
2002	Serena Williams USA
2003	Justine Henin-Hardenne BEL
2004	Anastasia Myskina RUS
2005	Justine Henin-Hardenne BEL
2006	Justine Henin-Hardenne BEL
2007	Justine Henin BEL
2008	Ana Ivanovic SER
2009	Svetlana Kuznetsova RUS
2010	Francesca Schiavone ITA
2011	Li Na CHN
2012	Maria Sharapova RUS
2013	Serena Williams USA

Australian Open – Men's Singles

1905	Rodney Heath AUS
1906	Tony Wilding NZL
1907	Horace Rice AUS
1908	Fred Alexander USA
1909	Tony Wilding NZL
1910	Rodney Heath AUS

1911	Norman Brookes AUS
1912	James Parke GBR
1913	Ernie Parker AUS
1914	Arthur O'Hara Wood AUS
1915	Gordon Lowe GBR
1916–18	*No competition*
1919	Algernon Kingscote GBR
1920	Pat O'Hara Wood AUS
1921	Rhys Gemmell AUS
1922	James Anderson AUS
1923	Pat O'Hara Wood AUS
1924	James Anderson AUS
1925	James Anderson AUS
1926	John Hawkes AUS
1927	Gerald Patterson AUS
1928	Jean Borotra FRA
1929	John Gregory GBR
1930	Edgar Moon AUS
1931	Jack Crawford AUS
1932	Jack Crawford AUS
1933	Jack Crawford AUS
1934	Fred Perry GBR
1935	Jack Crawford AUS
1936	Adrian Quist AUS
1937	Vivian McGrath AUS
1938	Donald Budge USA
1939	John Bromwich AUS
1940	Adrian Quist AUS
1941–45	*No competition*
1946	John Bromwich AUS
1947	Dinny Pails AUS
1948	Adrian Quist AUS
1949	Frank Sedgman AUS

1950	Frank Sedgman AUS
1951	Dick Savitt USA
1952	Ken McGregor AUS
1953	Ken Rosewall AUS
1954	Mervyn Rose AUS
1955	Ken Rosewall AUS
1956	Lew Hoad AUS
1957	Ashley Cooper AUS
1958	Ashley Cooper AUS
1959	Alex Olmedo USA
1960	Rod Laver AUS
1961	Roy Emerson AUS
1962	Rod Laver AUS
1963	Roy Emerson AUS
1964	Roy Emerson AUS
1965	Roy Emerson AUS
1966	Roy Emerson AUS
1967	Roy Emerson AUS
1968	Bill Bowrey AUS
1969	Rod Laver AUS
1970	Arthur Ashe USA
1971	Ken Rosewall AUS
1972	Ken Rosewall AUS
1973	John Newcombe AUS
1974	Jimmy Connors USA
1975	John Newcombe AUS
1976	Mark Edmondson AUS
1977	Roscoe Tanner USA
1977	Vitas Gerulaitis USA
1978	Guillermo Vilas ARG
1979	Guillermo Vilas ARG
1980	Brian Teacher USA
1981	Johan Kriek RSA

1982	Johan Kriek RSA
1983	Mats Wilander SWE
1984	Mats Wilander SWE
1985	Stefan Edberg SWE
1986	*No competition*
1987	Stefan Edberg SWE
1988	Mats Wilander SWE
1989	Ivan Lendl CZE
1990	Ivan Lendl CZE
1991	Boris Becker GER
1992	Jim Courier USA
1993	Jim Courier USA
1994	Pete Sampras USA
1995	Andre Agassi USA
1996	Boris Becker GER
1997	Pete Sampras USA
1998	Petr Korda CZE
1999	Yevgeny Kafelnikov RUS
2000	Andre Agassi USA
2001	Andre Agassi USA
2002	Thomas Johansson SWE
2003	Andre Agassi USA
2004	Roger Federer SUI
2005	Marat Safin RUS
2006	Roger Federer SUI
2007	Roger Federer SUI
2008	Novak Djokovic SRB
2009	Rafael Nadal ESP
2010	Roger Federer SUI
2011	Novak Djokovic SRB
2012	Novak Djokovic SRB
2013	Novak Djokovic SRB
2014	Stanislas Wawrinka SUI

Australian Open – Women's Singles

1922	Margaret Molesworth AUS
1923	Margaret Molesworth AUS
1924	Sylvia Lance AUS
1925	Daphne Akhurst AUS
1926	Daphne Akhurst AUS
1927	Esna Boyd AUS
1928	Daphne Akhurst AUS
1929	Daphne Akhurst AUS
1930	Daphne Akhurst AUS
1931	Coral Buttsworth AUS
1932	Coral Buttsworth AUS
1933	Joan Hartigan AUS
1934	Joan Hartigan AUS
1935	Dorothy Round GBR
1936	Joan Hartigan AUS
1937	Nancye Wynne AUS
1938	Dorothy Bundy USA
1939	Emily Westacott AUS
1940	Nancye Wynne AUS
1941–45	*No competition*
1946	Nancye Bolton AUS
1947	Nancye Bolton AUS
1948	Nancye Bolton AUS
1949	Doris Hart USA
1950	Louise Brough USA
1951	Nancye Bolton AUS
1952	Thelma Long AUS
1953	Maureen Connolly USA
1954	Thelma Long AUS
1955	Beryl Penrose AUS
1956	Mary Carter AUS
1957	Shirley Fry USA

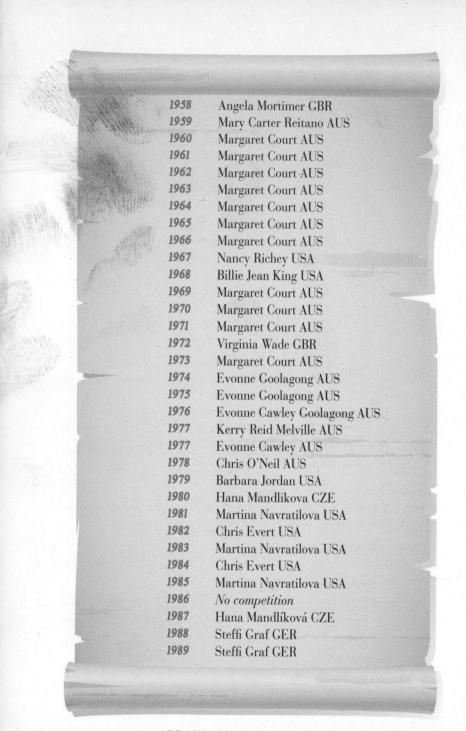

1958	Angela Mortimer GBR
1959	Mary Carter Reitano AUS
1960	Margaret Court AUS
1961	Margaret Court AUS
1962	Margaret Court AUS
1963	Margaret Court AUS
1964	Margaret Court AUS
1965	Margaret Court AUS
1966	Margaret Court AUS
1967	Nancy Richey USA
1968	Billie Jean King USA
1969	Margaret Court AUS
1970	Margaret Court AUS
1971	Margaret Court AUS
1972	Virginia Wade GBR
1973	Margaret Court AUS
1974	Evonne Goolagong AUS
1975	Evonne Goolagong AUS
1976	Evonne Cawley Goolagong AUS
1977	Kerry Reid Melville AUS
1977	Evonne Cawley AUS
1978	Chris O'Neil AUS
1979	Barbara Jordan USA
1980	Hana Mandlikova CZE
1981	Martina Navratilova USA
1982	Chris Evert USA
1983	Martina Navratilova USA
1984	Chris Evert USA
1985	Martina Navratilova USA
1986	*No competition*
1987	Hana Mandlíková CZE
1988	Steffi Graf GER
1989	Steffi Graf GER